Using Classroom Assessment to Improve Student Learning

Math problems aligned with NCTM and Common Core State standards

Professional Development Guide Included

Edited by

Anne M. Collins
Lesley University
Cambridge, Massachusetts

Writing Team

Antonia Cameron
Mathematics in the City
City College of New York
City University of New York
New York, New York

Jane Gawronski
San Diego State University (retired)
San Diego, California

Mary Eich
Newton Public Schools
Newton, Massachusetts

Sharon McCready
Nova Scotia Department of Education
Nova Scotia, Canada

D1082479

NCTM | NATIONAL COUNCIL OF TEACHERS OF MATHEMATICS

Library of Congress Cataloging-in-Publication Data

Using classroom assessment to improve student learning : math problems
aligned with NCTM and Common Core State standards
/ edited by Anne M. Collins ... [et al.].
    p. cm.
  Includes bibliographical references.
  ISBN 978-0-87353-660-8 (alk. paper)
  1. Mathematics—Study and teaching—United States—Evaluation. 2.
Mathematics—Study and teaching (Secondary)—Standards—United States.
3. Educational tests and measurements—United States. I. Collins, Anne
M., 1944–
  QA135.6.U85 2011
  510.71′273—dc22
                                                            2011003576

The National Council of Teachers of Mathematics is a public voice of mathematics
education, supporting teachers to ensure equitable mathematics learning of the
highest quality for all students through vision, leadership, professional development,
and research.

Printed in the United States of America

Contents

Preface

The National Council of Teachers of Mathematics asked our task force to compile a resource for classroom teachers that focuses on formative assessment and classroom practices aligned with *Curriculum Focal Points: A Quest for Coherence, Principles and Standards for School Mathematics,* and the *Common Core State Standards.* The National Mathematics Advisory Panel in 2008 cited scientific research linking improvement in student performance to effective implementation of formative assessment. The underlying premise was that national and state standards are the basis of the mathematics curriculum. Selecting rich problems, activities, and tasks that align with standards and frameworks is possibly one of the most challenging aspects of teaching mathematics. Assessing student understanding of the mathematics content involved in those tasks is another challenge that teachers face daily.

Linking assessment to everyday classroom instruction requires a shift in both thinking and practice. For many—educators, parents, students, politicians, and the media—the term *assessment* often means *score* or *grade.* The assessment they are thinking about is best described as assessment *of* learning, which traditionally does result in a grade or score. When thinking about assessment, many need to shift away from the ideas of tests, letter or numerical grades, or passing or failing as a means to flesh out a student's thinking and reasoning. When assessment focuses on evidence of student learning, teachers must work differently. Including anticipated student responses must become part of the planning for each lesson. To accommodate the various levels of understanding, you can examine the problem or task and revise it to furnish the necessary scaffolding that struggling students might need, as well as revising it to offer the challenges that students who demonstrate proficiency require.

We thank the following teachers and mathematics educators for allowing us into their classrooms: Katie Aspell, Andrew Barron, Linda Carnevale, Marria Carrington, Monica Clays, Linda Dacey, Jennifer DeThomas, Stephanie Gaeta, Jennifer Kesack, Debra Lancia, Ellen Lesiuk, Luis Martinez, Paul Mendo, Kim Morris, Donna Stouber, Jennifer Saarinen, Steve Yurek, and Tom Wyse. Only through their generosity could we work with their students, analyze student work, and evaluate mathematical thinking. We appreciate those who gave feedback on this project or helped us edit the manuscript.

We hope that you find our suggestions helpful as you move toward embedding formative assessment—assessment for learning—in your classrooms.

—The Writing Team

Introduction

FORMATIVE assessment is a key practice that, with effective implementation, positively affects students' achievement. A classroom environment that is conducive to effective formative assessment is one in which students

- feel safe to take risks while solving rich problems or tasks aligned with grade-level standards;
- are encouraged to work collaboratively;
- learn from one another and have the opportunity to share their work publicly as part of a community of discourse;
- have opportunities to reflect on and revise their mathematical writing and oral presentations to improve the clarity of their communication; and
- feel encouraged to work with each member of the community through the use of flexible grouping.

In such classrooms, teachers

- know the mathematics content and recognize key ideas and misconceptions;
- instruct students on appropriate protocols for working collaboratively in small groups;
- set clear expectations for student behaviors for individual and collaborative work;
- have the necessary tools to assess what their students know and can do;
- find ways to help students reflect on their problem solving, strategies, and writing to communicate with clarity; and
- know how to engage students in appropriate next steps effectively.

The description of the classroom environment that promotes effective formative assessment links back to the vision of school mathematics that opens *Principles and Standards for School Mathematics* (National Council of Teachers of Mathematics [NCTM] 2000):

> Imagine a classroom, a school, or a school district where all students have access to high-quality, engaging mathematics instruction. There are ambitious expectations for all, with accommodation for those who need it. Knowledgeable teachers have adequate resources to support their work and are continually growing as professionals. The curriculum is mathematically rich, offering students opportunities to learn important mathematical concepts and procedures with understanding. Technology is an essential component of the environment. Students confidently engage in complex mathematical tasks chosen carefully by teachers. They draw on knowledge from a wide variety of mathematical topics, sometimes approaching the same problem from different mathematical perspectives or representing the mathematics in different ways until they find methods that enable them to make progress. Teachers help students make, refine, and explore conjectures on the basis of evidence and use a variety of reasoning and proof techniques to confirm or dis-

prove those conjectures. Students are flexible and resourceful problem solvers. Alone or in groups and with access to technology, they work productively and reflectively, with the skilled guidance of their teachers. Orally and in writing, students communicate their ideas and results effectively. They value mathematics and engage actively in learning it. (p. 3)

This vision of mathematics teaching and learning describes an interactive process in which classes explore mathematical ideas in a social context, where the communication of mathematical thinking is an integral part of learning, and where "students confidently engage in complex mathematical tasks chosen carefully by teachers" (NCTM 2000, p. 3). It implies a more complex definition of mathematical proficiency than simply the ability to compute fluently and manipulate mathematical expressions.

What Is Mathematical Proficiency?

The National Research Council's *Adding It Up: Helping Children Learn Mathematics* describes mathematical proficiency as five interconnected strands (Kilpatrick, Swafford, and Findell 2001):

1. Conceptual understanding
2. Procedural fluency
3. Strategic competence
4. Adaptive reasoning
5. Productive disposition

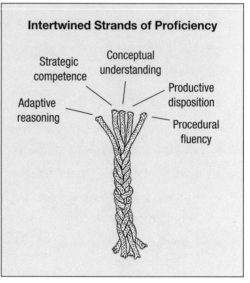

Intertwined Strands of Proficiency

Strategic competence

Conceptual understanding

Adaptive reasoning

Productive disposition

Procedural fluency

The strands of mathematical proficiency build a picture of a mathematically proficient student:

- Students with *conceptual understanding* know more than isolated facts and methods. They understand why a mathematical idea is important and the kinds of contexts in which it is useful.

- Students displaying *procedural fluency* know procedures and when to use them, and they can perform them flexibly, accurately, and efficiently.

- Students exhibiting *strategic competence* can formulate mathematical problems, represent them, and solve them.

- Students using *adaptive reasoning* can think logically about relationships among concepts and situations, consider alternatives, reason correctly, and justify conclusions.

- Students with a *productive disposition* see that mathematics makes sense and is both useful and worthwhile, believe that steady effort pays off, and see themselves as effective learners and doers of mathematics. (Kilpatrick, Swafford, and Findell 2001, chap. 4)

These strands—interwoven and interdependent—describe a set of knowledge, skills, abilities, and beliefs based on a body of research in cognitive psychology and mathematics education.

What Is Cognitive Demand?

Cognitive science studies how people learn. Levels of cognitive demand classify the kind of thinking that engaging with and solving a problem requires.

Until the middle of the twentieth century, the purpose of mathematics education for most people was to learn to compute accurately and efficiently. (Think of Bob Cratchit in Charles Dickens's *A Christmas Carol*, whom Ebenezer Scrooge employed to add long columns of numbers.) Elite institutions could produce the relatively few scientists and engineers needed for research and innovation—careers that required mathematical thinking. The emergence of computing technology during World War II, followed two decades later by the rapid growth of Asian science and engineering capabilities, has forced a long and highly emotional debate about the purpose of mathematics education and what mathematics is important for everyone to know and be able to do.

Part of the effort to define the characteristics of a new mathematics education system included the attempt to define exactly what kind of thinking children need to do as part of the learning process. Resnick described higher-order thinking in *Education and Learning to Think* (1987), when she proposed characteristics for the concept:

> Although we cannot define it exactly, we can recognize higher order thinking when it occurs. Consider the following:
>
> - Higher order thinking is *nonalgorithmic*. That is, the path of action is not fully specified in advance.
> - Higher order thinking tends to be *complex*. The total path is not "visible" (mentally speaking) from any single vantage point.
> - Higher order thinking often yields *multiple solutions*, each with costs and benefits, rather than unique solutions.
> - Higher order thinking involves *nuanced judgment* and interpretation.
> - Higher order thinking involves the application of *multiple criteria*, which sometimes conflict with one another.
> - Higher order thinking often involves *uncertainty*. Not everything that bears on the task at hand is known.
> - Higher order thinking involves *self-regulation* of the thinking process. We do not recognize higher order thinking in an individual when someone else "calls the plays" at every step.
> - Higher order thinking involves *imposing meaning*, finding structure in apparent disorder.
> - Higher order thinking is *effortful*. There is considerable mental work involved in the kinds of elaborations and judgments required. (pp. 2–3)

The Learning Research and Development Center at the University of Pittsburgh further developed these concepts in the early 1990s. The center sponsored the Quantitative Understanding: Amplifying Student Achievement and Reasoning (QUASAR) project with a grant from the Ford Foundation. QUASAR worked in Pittsburgh middle schools in a demonstration project aimed at raising low levels of student participation and performance in mathematics. They developed and implemented mathematics instructional programs based on three essential principles—that all students can (1) learn a broad range of mathematical content, (2) acquire a deeper and more meaningful understanding of mathematical ideas, and (3) demonstrate proficiency in mathematical reasoning and complex problem solving.

In the five years of the project, researchers developed the Mathematical Tasks Framework as a way to analyze classroom lessons. This framework identifies four levels of cognitive demand: memorization, procedures without connections, procedures with connections, and doing mathematics. Figure 1 describes each level.

Memorization tasks	**Procedures with connections tasks**
• involve either reproducing previously learned facts, rules, formulae, or definitions *or* committing facts, rules, formulae, or definitions to memory.	• focus students' attention on using procedures for developing deeper levels of understanding of mathematical concepts and ideas.
• cannot be solved using procedures because a procedure does not exist or because the time frame in which the task is being completed is too short to use a procedure.	• suggest pathways to follow (explicitly or implicitly) that are broad general procedures that have close connections to underlying conceptual ideas as opposed to narrow algorithms that are opaque with respect to underlying concepts.
• are not ambiguous—such tasks involve exact reproduction of previously seen material, and what is to be reproduced is clearly and directly stated.	• usually are represented in multiple ways (e.g., visual diagrams, manipulatives, symbols, problem situations). Making connections among multiple representations helps to develop meaning.
• have no connection to the concepts or meaning that underlie the facts, rules, formulae, or definitions being learned or reproduced.	• require some degree of cognitive effort. Although general procedures may be followed, they cannot be followed mindlessly. Students need to engage with the conceptual ideas that underlie the procedures to successfully complete the task and develop understanding.
Procedures without connections tasks	**Doing mathematics tasks**
• are algorithmic. Use of the procedure either is specifically called for or its use is evident based on prior instruction, experience, or placement of the task.	• requires complex and nonalgorithmic thinking (i.e., no predictable, well-rehearsed approach or pathway explicitly suggested by the task, task instructions, or a worked-out example is evident).
• require limited cognitive demand for successful completion. Little ambiguity exists about what needs to be done and how to do it.	• requires students to explore and understand the nature of mathematical concepts, processes, or relationships.
	• demands self-monitoring or self-regulation of one's own cognitive processes.

Fig. 1. Characteristics of mathematical tasks at the four levels of cognitive demand—*Continues*

Procedures without connections tasks	Doing mathematics tasks
• have no connection to the concepts or meaning that underlie the procedure being used. • are focused on producing correct answers rather than developing mathematical understanding. • require no explanations or offer only explanations that focus solely on describing the procedure that was used.	• requires students to access relevant knowledge and experiences and make appropriate use of them in working through the task. • requires students to analyze the task and actively examine task constraints that may limit possible solution strategies and solutions. • requires considerable cognitive effort and may involve some level of anxiety for the student owing to the unpredictable nature of the solution process required.

Fig. 1. Characteristics of mathematical tasks at the four levels of cognitive demand—*Continued*

"Doing mathematics tasks" is the highest level of cognitive demand and is closely related to the strands of strategic competence and adaptive reasoning that *Adding It Up* describes (Kilpatrick, Swafford, and Findell 2001). The NCTM Process Standards (NCTM 2000) further define the processes by which students "do math"—specific descriptions of the kinds of processes and habits of mind to integrate in our teaching to promote mathematical thinking that leads to proficiency (fig. 2).

Problem Solving

- Build new mathematical knowledge through problem solving.
- Solve problems that arise in mathematics and in other contexts.
- Apply and adapt a variety of appropriate strategies to solve problems.
- Monitor and reflect on the process of mathematical problem solving.

Reasoning and Proof

- Recognize reasoning and proof as fundamental aspects of mathematics.
- Make and investigate mathematical conjectures.
- Develop and evaluate mathematical arguments and proofs.
- Select and use various types of reasoning and methods of proof.

Communication

- Organize and consolidate their mathematical thinking through communication.
- Communicate their mathematical thinking coherently and clearly to peers, teachers, and others.
- Analyze and evaluate the mathematical thinking and strategies of others.
- Use the language of mathematics to express mathematical ideas precisely.

Fig. 2. NCTM Process Standards—*Continues*

Connections

- Recognize and use connections among mathematical ideas.

- Understand how mathematical ideas interconnect and build on one another to produce a coherent whole.

- Recognize and apply mathematics in contexts outside mathematics.

Representation

- Create and use representations to organize, record, and communicate mathematical ideas.

- Select, apply, and translate among mathematical representations to solve problems.

- Use representations to model and interpret physical, social, and mathematical phenomena.

Fig. 2. NCTM Process Standards—*Continued*

Teaching for Mathematical Proficiency

Resnick noted in the conclusion to her 1987 work,

> Thinking skills tend to be driven out of the curriculum by ever-growing demands for teaching larger and larger bodies of knowledge. The idea that knowledge must be acquired first and that its application to reasoning and problem solving can be delayed is a persistent one in educational thinking. "Hierarchies" of educational objectives, although intended to promote attention to higher order skills, paradoxically feed this belief by suggesting that knowledge acquisition is a first stage in a sequence of educational goals. The relative ease of assessing people's knowledge, as opposed to their thought processes, further feeds this tendency in educational practice. (pp. 48–49)

More than twenty years later, we still struggle to change an entrenched, traditional view of mathematics education and assessment that typically focuses on memorization and procedures without connections. We have all had the experience of teaching a mathematical procedure one day, being fairly certain that the lesson was successful and that most students could perform the procedure at the end of it, and realizing later that many of those same students have forgotten what they learned. Mathematical proficiency will not result from continual procedural instruction, nor will we know what kind of thinking students can do if we assess only their procedural knowledge.

Assessing Mathematical Proficiency

We are all familiar with summative assessments: the typical "math test" with problems that are easily marked correct or incorrect, that result in a grade, or that rank students in relation to other students.

However, we tend to be less familiar with formative assessments. Formative assessment is assessment *for* learning, whereas summative assessment is *of* learning. Formative assessments make students' thinking visible.

To provide learning experiences that build on and increase students' understanding—and to develop and deepen students' ability to reason and communicate mathematically—teachers must know what their students are thinking. Evidence from formative assessment allows the teacher to delve beneath students' factual knowledge to probe their depth of understanding. Formative assessment offers evidence of student learning that teachers can use to make informed decisions about the next question to ask and the next problem to assign or to determine which students to group together for the next mathematical task.

For instance, a student who demonstrated mastery in finding equivalent fractions was asked to name two fractions that come between $^3/_5$ and $^4/_5$. The student responded, "There are no fractions between 3 and 4." It appeared that the student understood equivalent fractions on the basis of a correct response to a summative question. But the response to the follow-up question, at a higher level of cognitive demand, indicated the student's limited understanding of fractions.

Exposing the depth of the student's understanding took only one good question—and this is the potential power of formative assessment. With the additional knowledge gathered from questions that cannot be answered by using a memorized fact or procedure, the teacher can differentiate instruction in the next lesson to extend each student's conceptual understanding of fractions and equivalent fractions with tasks that require more student thinking.

Overview of This Book

Chapter 1 includes general formative assessment information and strategies. Chapter 2 offers specific activities, protocols, and strategies for gathering evidence to help teachers make informed decisions about where in the learning progression their students are functioning. It will suggest ways to move students along their learning trajectory to attain the learning standards. Chapters 3–5 include formative assessment items, strategies, and protocols for the key mathematical ideas and connections from *Curriculum Focal Points: A Quest for Coherence* (NCTM 2006), all aligned with the Common Core State Standards for grades 6–8. The professional development guide outlines structures for workshops that can help teachers effectively use formative assessment in the mathematics classroom.

REFERENCES

Kilpatrick, Jeremy, Jane Swafford, and Bradford Findell, eds. *Adding It Up: Helping Children Learn Mathematics*. Washington, D.C.: National Academies Press, 2001.

National Council of Teachers of Mathematics (NCTM). *Principles and Standards for School Mathematics*. Reston, Va.: NCTM, 2000.

———. *Curriculum Focal Points for Prekindergarten through Grade 8 Mathematics: A Quest for Coherence*. Reston, Va.: NCTM, 2006.

Resnick, Lauren B. *Education and Learning to Think*. Washington, D.C.: National Academies Press, 1987.

Chapter 1
The Importance of Formative Assessment

When teachers understand what students know and can do, and then use that knowledge to make more effective instructional decisions, the net result is greater learning for students and a greater sense of satisfaction for teachers.
—Bright and Joyner (2005, p. 2)

What Is Formative Assessment, and Why Is It So Important?

FORMATIVE assessment is an ongoing process designed (*a*) to assess where a student is in the learning process and (*b*) to help a teacher use students' responses to determine the instructional activities necessary to further the student's learning. When we think about formative assessment, we must focus on the students and the activities in which the teacher daily engages them in the classroom (Wiliam 2007). The National Mathematics Advisory Panel (2008) cited research that confirms effective formative assessment's positive impact on students' achievement: "Formative assessment has been found to add the equivalent of two grades to students' achievement if done very well (Black and Wiliam 1998)."

Formative assessment is designed to make students' thinking visible. Teachers can gather information from observing and listening to students explain their reasoning and then make informed instructional decisions that go beyond students' initial responses to explore their underlying reasoning. For example, students may answer a question correctly, but without some aspect of formative assessment, a teacher may think that they understand the concept in question. Asking students to explain what they were thinking when solving the problem may reveal that they had appropriate procedural knowledge but not conceptual understanding and could not explain the mathematical ideas underlying why or how the procedure or algorithm worked.

When eighth-grade students were asked how to convert a base raised to a negative power to a base with a positive power, many students stated that "you just move the base from the numerator to the denominator and change the sign." When asked why, most of those same students replied, "Because that is the rule." Compare this response with that of a student who can explain the mathematics involved in this process. This student might begin by explaining that one cannot alter the value of the original fraction and so must identify an equivalent representation. The student most likely uses appropriate mathematical vocabulary to explain that multiplying the original expression by 1—the identity property of multiplication—does not change the value. The student may elaborate, adding that the value of 1 can take on a variety of representations, which depend on the situation. This student most likely will include a mathematical representation to support the oral explanation.

Formative assessment is one important component in the learning progression of students. It should be an integral part of classroom assessment practices. Unfortunately, many teachers overlook daily formative assessment, focusing mostly on summative assessments, such as weekly quizzes, chapter tests, annual state-mandated tests, the National Assessment of Educational Progress, the Trends in Mathematics and Science Study, and other standardized tests. Such assessments actually do little to influence students' learning because they do little to influence teachers' practice. Summative assessments do have their place in the educational process and assessment system, but these tests—which are so far removed from students' daily experiences—do not affect students in real time. Every classroom must institute appropriate, daily formative assessments, since it is formative assessment that touches students on an ongoing basis, in real time, and has the power to effect students' achievement because it has the potential to develop and deepen their thinking.

Margaret Heritage, of the Assessment and Accountability Comprehensive Center, shares a graphic (fig. 1.1) to show how various assessments affect students. It illustrates how assessments that are removed from students' regular interaction have less influence on students' learning progressions.

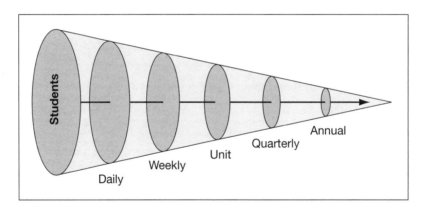

Fig. 1.1. How various assessments affect students

What happens daily is closest to students and has the greatest effect on them. This finding translates to the most important component of formative assessment: "What happens in the classroom has the greatest impact on student learning" (Heritage 2008). Notice how far away from the student the quarterly and annual assessments are located. The farther away from the student, the less likely the assessment is to have an immediate impact on the student's learning.

Many districts are now implementing benchmark assessments designed to inform district administrators about the progress students are making in mathematics. But take caution with these assessments: most benchmark assessments are better suited for instructional program decisions. For instance, a quarterly assessment may inform the school or district about the alignment of the textbook with the standards, whether a concept has been taught, or what skills students have solving unique problems when the teacher cannot offer suggestions or help. One effective use of the benchmark assessments is to identify students who may be at risk. However, a significant limitation is that the benchmark results do not suggest how best the school or teacher should intervene in working effectively with those at-risk students. Also, these district-developed benchmark assessments often do not meet even minimum validity evidence (Shepard 2005).

What Does Formative Assessment Look Like in the Classroom?

Formative assessment varies and is ongoing. But effective formative assessment will do the following:

- Elicit evidence about students' learning
- Give teachers and students feedback about students' learning
- Provide information so that teachers can adjust instruction in real time
- Allow time for students' self-reflection
- Involve students actively in their learning

Effective formative assessment is not a one-size-fits-all concept. Rather, formative assessment includes a variety of practices designed to help the teacher understand what students think; how they reason through problems; the depth of their conceptual understanding as well as procedural competency; their proficiency in communicating mathematically, symbolically, orally, and in writing; their ability to work collaboratively; and the prior knowledge they bring to a concept and their ability to build on that prior knowledge. Most important, formative assessment is not something that teachers do *to* students; rather, it actively engages students in the process of their own learning. It empowers students to take control over their learning. Equally important: the assessment is built into the lesson planning.

Teachers' Role in Formative Assessment

Competency with mathematics content is a primary consideration for effective instruction and assessment. To be effective, middle school teachers of mathematics must have both conceptual and procedural mathematics content knowledge that goes beyond the grades they teach. Equally important is the need for the pedagogical content knowledge that will enable them to teach the conceptual and procedural content effectively to every student in the class. As teachers everywhere struggle to close the achievement gap, we acknowledge the need for teaching proficiencies with the following:

- The mathematical underpinnings of formulas and procedures that explain why they work
- The future mathematics for which the current mathematics lays the foundation
- Using many different representations of concepts and procedures
- Recognizing and encouraging deep thinking in classroom discussions

Assessing prior knowledge

Teachers must also have knowledge of the students they teach, how much mathematical knowledge the students have, and how students use that knowledge. Consider the following: *Stephen was heard explaining to his mother that he didn't need to go to school until November. When his mother asked why, Stephen explained, "All we do is repeat what we learned last year, and I remember all that stuff. We don't learn anything new until November."*

Assessing students' prior knowledge is a crucial component in determining whether a need exists to pose more challenging problems, more scaffolded problems, or both. Since learning is developmental, not everyone is in the same place at the same time. Students' marking time and waiting for others to catch up is not appropriate, nor is teaching at a level beyond their comprehension. Including *range questions* in your lessons—questions designed to identify students' mathematical development—is one way teachers can accurately determine where students are in the learning progression. Often the results of a range question dictate the need to differentiate instruction.

Giving feedback to teachers and students

The power of feedback is one facet of formative assessment that surprises many teachers. To use feedback effectively, all parties must agree on exactly what constitutes feedback. Wiggins (2004) states that "feedback is information about how we did in light of some goal." It is useful information about how students solved a problem. Some feedback might be a question asked to a student engaged in a task. Other feedback may be written—for instance, a sticky note on a paper that poses a question for a student to reflect on. Feedback should not be labor intensive but rather a natural extension of our interactions with students. It is not evaluative, so we do not need to worry about recording a grade. Feedback is an important component in our goal of improving students' learning.

Research has shown that when students receive a graded paper, they look at the grade; often if the grade is good, they bring the paper home, but if it is not good many middle school students crumple it up and throw it away. When they receive a grade together with feedback on individual questions, students typically respond in the same fashion. However, when they receive feedback without a grade, students not only read the comments but often respond to the feedback. Giving students *neutral* and *descriptive feedback* usually results in their making more thoughtful responses and, by design, helps students reflect on their work. Neutral feedback includes asking students to explain their thinking further, such as asking, "What might happen if . . ." or "Will that always work?" Effective descriptive feedback gives students an idea of what they are doing well, informs them on how what they are doing links to classroom learning, and offers specific input on what they must do next to advance in their learning.

You might think about an assessment sandwich. The sandwich consists of a positive comment, followed by a clarifying question or comment written to help the student meet a standard, followed by an encouraging comment. Effective feedback is also a way to challenge thinking, support generalizations of mathematical ideas, and help students communicate with clarity. Neutral and descriptive feedback are both powerful tools in motivating students and helping them move forward in reaching the next goal in their learning progression.

Students' Role in Formative Assessment

To really succeed, however, students must learn to self-assess so that they can understand the main purposes of their learning and thereby grasp what they need to do to achieve.

—Black and Wiliam (1998, p. 12)

For formative assessment to affect students' achievement positively, students must be actively involved in the process. By the middle grades, students should be able to articulate areas in which they are proficient and those in which they need more support. Students should be expected to maintain a record of their performance. Although the concept is novel for most middle schoolers, teachers should encourage students and give them time to reflect on their achievement. When students are actively engaged in criteria and goal setting, self-reflection and self-evaluation are the next logical steps in the learning process. "Without time to reflect on and interact meaningfully with new information, students are unlikely to retain much of what is 'covered' in their classrooms" (Dodge 2009, p. 4).

Since teaching is ultimately about student learning, stating that "I taught it, they just didn't get it" is unacceptable. Rather, finding a method to engage students in a way that makes them accountable for their own learning is appropriate. An important part of this endeavor is to engage students in developing the criteria and goal setting. When students are engaged in setting goals, they have a better opportunity to understand the teacher's expectations. When you share exemplar work illustrating your expectations, students are more likely to understand where they are and where they are expected to be. When students share their own work in the classroom community, when they have to defend their ideas publicly, they develop more effective ways of communicating their reasoning both orally and in writing. A collaborative effort by both you and students enhances both the teaching and the learning that occur in the classroom community.

Students often need assistance getting started in self-reflection. Asking students specific questions is often helpful for getting them to focus on what it is they are reflecting. Some suggestions:

- Describe the strategies you used to solve this problem. What other strategies might you use the next time you solve a similar problem?
- Did you receive feedback during the problem-solving process? If so, was it helpful? Explain how it helped you.
- Did you collaborate with peers when you were solving this problem? Was the collaboration helpful? If so, how? If not, why not?

If you are asking students to complete a portfolio, you may want to add the following types of questions as the students reflect on their progress:

- Why did you choose these entries?

- Which portfolio entry represents your best work? Why do you think so?

- Which portfolio entries represent the most mathematical growth? How do they show your growth in understanding?

- Which entries represent problems or tasks that you found most challenging? Explain those challenges.

Since one tenet of formative assessment includes students' taking responsibility for their own learning, it follows that these students participate in student-led parent–teacher conferences. By engaging students in discussing their work, you are actually empowering them to take responsibility for their progress and giving them a forum in which to display all that they have learned. These conferences should not be punitive; rather, they should be experiences in which the students have an opportunity to showcase their mathematical progress.

REFERENCES

Black, Paul, and Dylan Wiliam. "Assessment and Classroom Learning." *Assessment in Education: Principles, Policy, and Practice* 5 (March 1998): 7–74.

Bright, George W., and Jeane M. Joyner. "Dynamic Classroom Assessment: Linking Mathematical Understanding to Instruction." ETA Cuisenaire. 2005. www.etacuisenaire.com/professionaldevelopment/math/dca/dynamic.jsp (accessed September 9, 2010).

Dodge, Judith. "What Are Formative Assessments and Why Should We Use Them?" *25 Quick Formative Assessments for a Differentiated Classroom.* New York: Scholastic, 2009.

Heritage, Margaret. "Formative Assessment." Presented at the annual meeting of the Association of State Supervisors of Mathematics, Salt Lake City, Utah, April 5, 2008.

National Mathematics Advisory Panel. *Foundations for Success: The Final Report of the National Mathematics Advisory Panel.* Washington, D.C.: U.S. Department of Education, 2008.

Shepard, Lorrie A. "Competing Paradigms of Classroom Assessment: Echoes of the Tests-and-Measurement Model." Presented at the annual meeting of the American Educational Research Association, Montreal, April 2005.

Wiggins, Grant. "Assessment as Feedback." New Horizons for Learning. 2004. www.newhorizons.org/strategies/assess/wiggins.htm.

Wiliam, Dylan. "Keeping Learning on Track: Formative Assessment and the Regulation of Learning." In *Second Handbook of Mathematics Teaching and Learning,* edited by Frank K. Lester Jr., pp. 1053–98. Greenwich, Conn.: Information Age Publishing, 2007.

Chapter 2
Classroom Practices

To be formative, assessment must include a recipe for future action.

—Dylan Wiliam

PRINCIPLES and Standards for School Mathematics (National Council of Teachers of Mathematics [NCTM] 2000) identifies both Content Standards and Process Standards. The Process Standards require students to "discuss and validate their mathematical thinking, create and analyze a variety of representations that illuminate the connections within the mathematics, and apply the mathematics that they are learning in solving problems, judging claims, and making decisions" (NCTM 2006, p. 8).

NCTM also developed Curriculum Focal Points to focus instruction in each grade level, K–8, on three key mathematical ideas. *Curriculum Focal Points for Prekindergarten through Grade 8 Mathematics: A Quest for Coherence* (NCTM 2006) further develops the three key ideas for each grade level through connections to other identified mathematical strands. *Curriculum Focal Points* locates the mathematics for each grade firmly in contexts that promote the Process Standards: problem solving, reasoning, communication, making connections, and designing and analyzing representations.

The Common Core State Standards (Common Core State Standards Initiative [CCSSI] 2008) were developed to standardize mathematical practices and learning standards across the country. The National Governors Association in conjunction with the Council of Chief State School Officers oversaw this national initiative. The standards articulate grade-level learning goals, as well as different pathways of focus for high school students.

Implicit in both *Principles and Standards* and *Curriculum Focal Points* is that important concepts should be taught deeply and taught well. Students are expected to think—to be engaged in solving problems that address grade-level topics at high levels of cognitive demand.

Crucial to such instruction is teachers' knowledge of what students know about the concept to be taught. Using formative assessment in the classroom is a natural extension for understanding what students know and can do, as well as how well they can communicate mathematics verbally and symbolically. The nine formative assessment strategies and tools in this chapter allow you to gather quick but accurate information about your students' understandings, misconceptions, and challenges linked to particular mathematical goals. Figure 2.1 aligns the strategies with their assessment goals.

Assessment's Purpose	Formative Assessment	Strategies and Tools
Determine the range of understanding within a class of a concept before instruction	Assessing prior knowledge	Range questions
Record evidence of students' proficiency in problem solving, computation, and communication, as well as their work ethic and disposition toward learning	Assessing students at work	Observation protocols
Make students' thinking visible		Gallery walks
		Round-robin activities; accountable talk
Make students' thinking available to the teacher and peers, and respond to students' ideas or strategies	Probing students' thinking	Mathematical discourse: accountable talk and the math congress
		Hinge questions; focused questions
Determine what individual students are thinking		Interviews or conferences
Give students neutral or descriptive information	Using assessment to plan instruction	Neutral feedback
Assess what students learned in a lesson before planning the next lesson		Exit cards (exit slips)

Fig. 2.1. Aligning strategies with assessment goals

Toolkit for Formative Assessment

Identifying tools that make assessment for learning practical is a vital step in implementing daily formative assessments. Formative assessment, when well designed and implemented, enables you to develop instructional activities for the specific needs of your students, to make adjustments as students progress through a unit of study, and to give all students appropriately challenging mathematical tasks. Unlike summative assessment, formative assessment is often "invisible" to the students because it is part of daily classroom interactions, is frequent and quick, takes place while students are working, and does not result in a grade.

The nine classroom strategies and tools we describe here allow you to gather evidence about your students' understandings, misconceptions, and challenges in an interactive, low-stress setting. Many of the practices require you to think differently about how you engage your students in doing mathematics and how you determine daily instructional goals and activities. Teachers have implemented each identified practice in classrooms, and both teachers and students found the practices effective. We highlight nine formative assessment tools:

1. Range questions
2. Observation protocols
3. Gallery walks
4. Round-robin activities
5. Focused questions and hinge questions
6. Interviews
7. Mathematical discourse—accountable talk and math congress
8. Neutral feedback
9. Exit cards (exit slips)

Gather Evidence about Students' Understanding

Our overarching goal is to engage students in work that will help them develop proficiency in mathematics. Students who struggle to understand the relevance of mathematics in the world and in their own lives—constantly asking "why are we doing this?"—tend to be doing worksheet- and textbook-driven mathematics focused on procedural skills with low levels of cognitive demand. Assessments based on the worksheet model produce evidence of students' ability to complete worksheets and problems from textbooks. Students who have adapted to a worksheet-driven instructional model can test well on procedural skills yet still not have a deep understanding of concepts.

Conversely, in classrooms where teachers assign mathematically rich, interesting problems and encourage student interactions around mathematics, students challenge each other while modeling mathematics, making predictions, formulating conjectures, and experimenting with physical data. They represent those data in tables, charts, or graphs, complete with appropriate equations or justifications. These students are doing math: using procedural skills in the service of mathematics with a high level of cognitive demand. They work in the realm of process skills, using higher-order thinking skills as they work on complex mathematical tasks at the appropriate level of challenge. In this model, you must continually gather evidence of students' understandings to ensure that each student meets the curricular standards and understands the essential concepts.

The interactions among students as they do math may result in a classroom that does not conform to the traditional image of a mathematics classroom, but without interaction, the level of cognitive demand will remain low. The formative assessment strategies and tools we discuss are well suited to the latter instructional model and will facilitate an "orderly chaos" in which you will be able to gather evidence about students' performance.

Assessing prior knowledge: Range questions

Awareness of what a child knows and understands is the first step in planning instruction designed to deepen that knowledge and understanding. Before assigning a problem, you must identify the standard or focal point with which the item is aligned. Thinking reflectively about the item's pivotal concept is also appropriate. You also need to know about the key misconceptions and challenges that many students share and to consider whether the question presents a low, medium, or high level of cognitive demand.

After reflecting on those components, you are ready to identify questions to ask before the lesson begins to assess students' prior knowledge. Range questions (Heritage 2008) are posed at the beginning of a lesson to determine students' scope of understanding. These questions are designed to be quick—no more than five minutes—and you can post them in the classroom as students enter or as they begin their mathematics lesson. Range questions should be relevant to that day's lesson concept. Most important, range questions are starting points for solving problems and often lead to pivotal understandings. Sample range questions include the following:

- Name two fractions that have a value greater than $2/7$.
- Name two fractions that have a value less than $2/7$.
- Tell me what you see: $3/4$
- Turn to your partner and tell him or her everything you can about $y = -3x + 4$.
- In what order would you place the following fractions on a number line? $3/4$, $5/8$, $2/5$, $1/2$
- Show me about how long 5 centimeters is.
- What do you know about the multiples of 6?
- If you collect a penny a day, how long do you think it will take to collect a million pennies? A billion pennies?

These questions are broad, allow for more than one answer, and require students to share their thinking.

Part of the planning for any lesson involves identifying a problem that you can adjust to meet the needs of all students. Students who answer the range question with strong mathematical reasoning need a problem that enriches their knowledge, deepens their understanding, and moves them forward in their learning. Students who do not answer correctly or who exhibit uncertainty about their response may require a version of the problem designed to support and solidify their knowledge. Still others may need more scaffolding to begin to think about the same problem. This scaffolding could be as simple as breaking down components of the problem by using bullets to help the students focus on one part of the problem at a time.

Range questions with specific tasks for each grade are in chapters 3–5. You can find more generic range questions in Marian Small and Amy Lin's 2010 book *More Good Questions: Great Ways to Differentiate Secondary Mathematics Instruction.*

Assessing students at work: Observation protocols

As anyone who has taught middle school knows, students at this age want to be physically active and talk with their classmates. In fact, research suggests that they *need* to move around and converse with one another. Classrooms with successful students routinely have students who are out of their seats modeling mathematics, making predictions, formulating conjectures, and experimenting with physical data—which they then organize in tables, charts, or graphs, complete with appropriate equations or justifications.

As long as you establish norms and expectations for behavior, you can harness and incorporate into daily classroom routines this need for movement and interaction, which makes a traditional teaching style difficult. Teachers who involve their students in developing classroom protocols complete with posted rubrics detailing classroom expectations typically have fewer problems with classroom management and behavior.

You can use one such protocol, observation, to gather evidence about students' proficiency in problem solving, computation, and communication, as well as about their disposition toward mathematics. This protocol's focus depends on the criteria you set for your students. If, while your students are working collaboratively, they must share problem-solving strategies, communicate orally and symbolically, compute with or without a calculator, justify their answers, or report on their findings, you can design the observation protocol to record each student's level of competence in those areas. If you are concerned about knowing when a particular student gets frustrated and gives up, you can include that category in the protocol and keep a record of whether the student's tolerance improves as he or she becomes more confident with the mathematics.

Observational protocols, when well designed and carefully recorded, serve as records of students' progress and give you evidence on which to base instructional decisions.

Practicing teachers wrote the protocols in figures 2.2 and 2.3 to document their students' mathematics proficiency, habits of mind, and mathematical confidence. Each reflects the teacher's understanding of the many elements of mathematical proficiency. The teachers used the completed forms as evidence when interviewing their students. Another teacher found the observational protocol in figure 2.3 better suited to her teaching style.

Assessing students at work: Gallery walks

Sharing students' work is an important component of a community of learners. Gallery walks offer students a forum in which they can rotate among various stations where they can post a comment, strategy, question, or solution. While students are working their way through the stations, you listen for appropriate mathematical terminology, listen for mathematical arguments, and watch for appropriate symbolic notation. If, for example, students are working on a geometry unit that requires understanding geometric vocabulary, you might design a gallery walk with eight or ten stations. Each station could have a geometric term written on large poster paper. Students, in small groups, rotate among the stations, posting their definition of each term. A class discussion may follow that compares the definitions and lets students agree on an accurate mathematical definition.

Fig. 2.2. Sample observational protocol

Concept	Behaviors and effort				Group work				Learning and understanding									Comments
Student name	On task	Asks topical questions	Answers questions	Takes notes	Active participant	Copies work from others	Helps others	Accepts help	Accurately applies concepts	Multiple representations	Multiple strategies	Explains process: writing (W), verbal (V), both (B)	Applies previously learned concepts	Correct answer	Computational accuracy	Procedural accuracy	Problem-solving strategies	

Fig. 2.3. Another sample observational protocol

Skill	Learning and understanding									Student habits	Comments
	Opening activity		Work time							On task	
Student name	Active learner	Understands question(s)	Shows work (computation diagram, table, graph, equation)	Explains solution	Are the answers accurate?	Group work	Accountable talk	Completes work	Help		

A well-organized gallery walk promotes critical thinking; written expression; oral communication; and an interactive, student-centered environment. Assign students problems that require them to analyze, predict, compare, construct, or justify so that, after they complete the mathematics, a rich discussion can follow. After posting their work, students should expect to justify their thinking, field questions from their classmates, and make connections between their work and previous mathematical experiences—all features of mathematical tasks at a high level of cognitive demand.

Gallery walks can serve as formative assessments, with teachers using an observation protocol to record students' involvement. You can also use gallery walks more formally as summative assessments by posting rubrics before students begin the process. You must be clear on the gallery walk's purpose before beginning one. If the gallery walk is designed as formative assessment, you should listen to students as they discuss their work. If you have designed the gallery walk as summative assessment, in which students are graded, students must know in advance about how you will grade the work. Many teachers find that involving the students in developing the rubrics that identify exemplary work is most effective.

Gallery walks have the flexibility of working effectively in as little as fifteen minutes or to allow a forum in which students may present a unit project over days or weeks. The gallery walk at the end of a unit might showcase students' culminating activity. It may include a collage to exhibit students' favorite numbers and all the mathematical information they learned about them, or it may include illustrations of exponential growth or decay, or the design for a community playground (Lappan 2006). Such a gallery walk may be timed to coincide with parent–teacher conferences, family math nights, or open houses to allow students to display their work to an audience outside their classroom.

Students can also assess the success of the gallery walk. You can use the students' reflection evaluation in figure 2.4 to determine how well you structured the gallery walk.

	General Observation	Disagree		Neutral		Agree
1	The directions for the gallery walk were clear. I knew what do to successfully complete a gallery walk.	1	2	3	4	5
2	The topics in the gallery walk were interesting to me.	1	2	3	4	5
3	We worked more collaboratively in the gallery walk than we do with usual class discussion techniques.	1	2	3	4	5
4	During the gallery walk, all group members participated and listened respectfully to one another.	1	2	3	4	5

Fig. 2.4. A gallery walk evaluation form for students—*Continues*

	General Observation	Disagree		Neutral		Agree
5	I felt I gained a better understanding of the topic if I learned the topic through lecture. (Explain your answer.)	1	2	3	4	5
6	The wording of gallery walk questions was clear. If not, which questions needed improvement? Question 1 2 3 4 5	1	2	3	4	5
7	I felt we had enough time to discuss each topic at learning stations.	1	2	3	4	5
8	The gallery walk was easy to use.	1	2	3	4	5
9	The evaluation criteria (how I will be graded) for the gallery walk were clear.	1	2	3	4	5
10	My overall experience with the gallery walk was satisfactory.	1	2	3	4	5
11	I would like to participate in another gallery walk.	1	2	3	4	5

Fig. 2.4. A gallery walk evaluation form for students—*Continued*

One Monday, a teacher concerned about the potential chaos of a gallery walk decided to be adventurous. She assigned a gallery walk to gather evidence about her students' understanding of mathematical vocabulary terms. She posted the mathematical terms *profit, income,* and *expense.* After reading the students' definitions, she realized that most of her students truly had not mastered these terms' meanings. She spent the week working on those concepts, through problem solving, and on Friday revisited the terms in a *gallery run.* A gallery run operates the same way as the gallery walk, except that it gives students only half the time to complete the activity. Figures 2.5–7 show this gallery run's results. The teacher was pleasantly surprised with the progress her students displayed, but she also documented that some misconceptions remained.

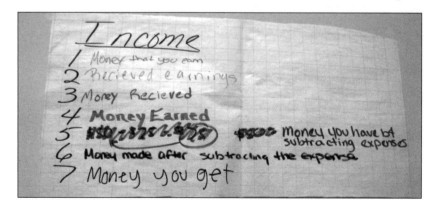

Fig. 2.5. Students' definitions of *income* from the gallery run

Most groups appear to understand the meaning of *income*; however, two posts appear to offer evidence of confusion between *profit* and *income*. Some groups described *income* as money received rather than earned, or money you get but no indication of how you get it. These statements warrant further discussion.

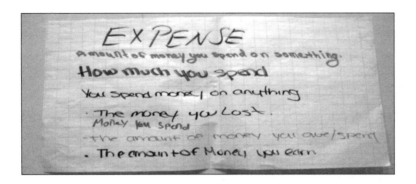

Fig. 2.6. Students' definitions of *expense* from the gallery run

Most students defined *expense* as an amount of money spent on certain goods. Yet one group of students referred to an amount of money "lost"—this comment needs further discussion. Also, notice the last comment: "The amount of money you earn." This group of students misunderstands *expense*, and further discussion is appropriate.

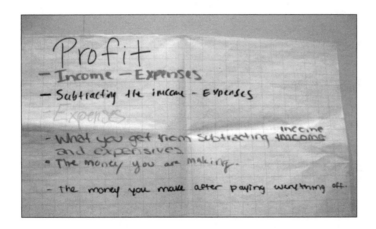

Fig. 2.7. Students' definitions of *profit* from the gallery run

Students also varied in their definitions of *profit*. Some evident conceptual misunderstandings include defining profit as "expenses" and "the money you are making."

Going by the results posted in the gallery run, the teacher decided to continue including problems involving profit, expense, and income in her range questions, exit cards, and homework assignments. She also decided that the gallery walk was so successful that she would use it to share students' problem solving.

Assessing students at work: Round-robin activities

Middle school students are expected to master the order of operations, simplifying expressions, and solving multistep equations, among other procedural skills that both *Curriculum Focal Points* and *Principles and Standards* identify. Students need time to develop proficiency with these mathematical skills and procedures as well as with conceptual understanding. One lesson with homework will not be enough to develop deep understanding for any student. Engaging students in interactive activities allows them to explore ideas from varied entry points and mathematical preparation, holds their interest longer, and is more effective than assigning worksheets.

The round-robin activity is designed to allow you to assess students while they work. It also lets you intervene as needed before any misconception or procedural misstep can germinate.

Here's how you run a round robin. Group students into threes, with each group member assigned the number 1, 2, or 3. Instruct each student who is a number 1 to go to the board. Dictate an expression or equation for that student to record. On completion of the dictation, student number 1 does one step and then sits down. Student 2 goes up to the board, does step 2, and then sits down. Student 3 follows student 2 to the board and does step 3. This process continues until the computation is complete (fig. 2.8).

All students assigned the number 1 go to the board and write:	$16 - 3(17 - 4 \times 3) + 5$
Student 1 does one step:	$16 - 3(17 - 12) + 5$
Student 2 takes over and does one step:	$16 - 3(5) + 5$
Student 3 takes over and does one step:	$16 - 15 + 5$
Student 1 returns and does one step:	$1 + 5$
Student 2 completes the computation:	6

Fig. 2.8. The round-robin approach

The formative assessment component is a seamless part of the activity. Observe each group at the board. If a student erred in the first step and wrote $13(17 - 4 \times 3) + 5$, you would sidle up to the student and quietly ask where the 13 came from. You might ask the student to list the order in which the operations are done or to name the terms in the problem. You may highlight that the 3 is a factor and ask what the second factor is. The important part is ensuring that the student does not make a conceptual error without immediate intervention. Often during the round robin, students help their teammates if they see an error, so the formative assessment is about peers helping peers.

After one computation is complete, instruct the students with the number 2 to go to the board. Dictate another problem, and have student 2 do the first step, followed by student 3, and then student 1.

For solving multistep equations, ask the students not only to complete one step of the procedure but also to identify the mathematical property the student used (fig. 2.9)

You dictate $3a + 7 - 5a = 2(4a - 3) + 2a$.

The first student may record $7 - 2a = 2(4a - 3) + 2a$ (combine like terms).

The next student may record $7 - 2a = 8a - 6 + 2a$ (distributive property).

The next student may record $7 - 2a = 10a - 6$ (combine like terms).

The next student may record $7 - 2a + 2a = 10a - 6 + 2a$ (additive inverse).

The next student may record $7 + 6 = 12a - 6 + 6$ (additive inverse).

The next student may record $13 \div 12 = 12a \div 12$ (multiplicative inverse).

The next student may record $^{13}/_{12} = a$.

Fig. 2.9. The round robin for a multistep problem

The round-robin technique offers several advantages:

- It shows how well students can enter a problem-solving process at various decision points.
- It actively engages all students in problem solving.
- It fosters collaborative work among students' peers.
- It gives the class the opportunity to work through many different problems within a short period.
- It reinforces students' skills in a nonthreatening environment.

Probing students' thinking: Focused questions

Think for a moment about how you ask your students a question during a whole-class discussion. Do you pose a question, call on one student to answer the question, and then move on after the student answers or you get a correct answer? This typical method of questioning is actually a conversation between two people—you and the student asked to respond. Students not involved in the conversation don't have to think.

Or do you pose a question, directing your students to think about the question individually for a minute or two before instructing them to turn to their partner and discuss the question? After a specified wait time, do you ask a representative from each pair or small group to report their responses? This method of questioning is often referred to as *active listening* or *think-pair share*. Such an approach engages all students. All students think about a question, discuss the question with their peers, and finally report their responses.

A conjecture is similar to a hypothesis in science: an idea that is tested, revised, and retested. The teacher often records on a conjecture board the various responses students offer from range questions, problems, or suggested algorithms. Think of the conjecture board as a parking lot—a location designated for recording student ideas. As students work through their mathematics lesson, teachers encourage them to think about whether the conjecture is always mathematically true, test the conjecture, revise it when and if the original conjecture is inaccurate, remove it if someone gives a counterexample or a negation, and then test the revised conjecture. One teacher reports that her students worked harder to find a negation or counterexample to the posted conjectures than they did on their assigned work. She includes the conjecture board in her daily lessons.

Probing students' thinking: Hinge questions

Bright and Joyner (2005) discuss three different types of questions to ask students when they are working individually or in pairs or small groups: engaging questions, clarifying questions, and refocusing questions.

Heritage (2008) refers to hinge questions in addition to the earlier range questions. Hinge questions depend on what students are saying or doing. Similar to Bright and Joyner's conceptual model, hinge questions might involve engaging, refocusing, or clarifying questions. The type of question teachers ask depends on what is happening with the students at various times throughout the lesson.

Even so, you must anticipate the questions you think might arise and have a small battery of relevant engaging, refocusing, and clarifying questions ready before you ask students to work the problem. The best questions take thought. You might come up with one spontaneously, but a little planning will give you a better chance to get the most out of the teachable moment when it arises.

Engaging questions

Engaging questions are fairly easy to ask if students are working on an interesting problem. These questions are designed to engage students with the problem. You can ask engaging questions during the problem-solving process when a student stops participating and needs a nudge to return to work on the assigned problem. The problem or task should be interesting and appropriate for the particular grade level. A well-thought-out engaging question should spark students' interest and make them want to solve the problem.

The following problem often intrigues middle school students and lends itself to asking engaging, refocusing, and clarifying questions: *If you begin counting your heartbeats at exactly twelve o'clock New Year's Day, when will your heart have beaten 1 million times? Support your answer.* Think about this problem. It's a straightforward problem that interests most students. Why is it interesting? What are the mathematical concepts behind it? What information do your students need to consider? How might your students begin? Would you ask your students to make a prediction before you instructed them to work on finding a solution? Would you invite students to work in pairs or small groups to solve the problem?

Some engaging questions appropriate for this problem include the following: *Do you think each member of your group has the same heart rate? How can you determine each person's heart rate? How can you incorporate each person's heart rate in your solution?* These questions are designed to guide students toward thinking about taking one another's pulse and using the data to find an average. If students did determine the mean heart rate, two follow-up engaging questions might be *What would happen if you used the median class heart rate?* and *How would your results differ?*

Now, compare the question about heart rates to a more typical question students are asked, which includes the same basic mathematical processes: *Compute 1,000,000 ÷ 72.*

Which question is more likely to appeal to students? More important, which solution process allows you to ask engaging questions and yields evidence about students' conceptual understanding and procedural skills?

Refocusing questions

Refocusing questions prevent students from pursuing a dead-end strategy when solving a particular problem, guide students to answer the question asked, and return them to the task at hand if they drift off. A refocusing question would be appropriate if students are using just one person's heart rate. For example, *I noticed that you have already started doing calculations that involve multiplication. Can you explain to me what the calculations represent? How will they help you find out how many times a heart beats every hour?*

Clarifying questions

Clarifying questions ask students to explain what they are thinking or to clarify the assignment or directions. For this problem, clarifying questions might include the following: *Are you sure everyone in your group has the same heart rate? Do you think your heart rate stays the same all day? How is multiplying your heart rate by 60 seconds in a minute different from dividing your heart rate by 60 seconds in a minute? Which do you think will best help you begin to determine when your heart rate beats the millionth time? What were you thinking when you multiplied 1 million by 60 seconds in a minute? If your heart beats 72 times per minute, how many times will it beat in 2 minutes? 3 minutes? 10 minutes?* Each question focuses on making students' thinking visible.

Probing student thinking: Interviews and conferences

A natural follow-up to the questioning process is the interview. Teachers interview individual students to ensure exact understanding of what students are thinking about their problem solving. Interviews should take place outside the mathematics class time in a quiet area where the student can feel relaxed and comfortable. Setting the environment for the interview is important to reassure students that the interview is not punitive but rather to give the teacher insights about the students' thinking to better meet their learning needs.

A grade 7 teacher assigned the following problem to her students as a range question: *A photograph that is 6 inches on the base and 8 inches high is to be enlarged so that the new base is to be 15 inches. What will the height of the enlargement be?*

She instructed her students to predict the length of the enlarged photograph without using paper or pencil. She recorded the range of answers on the board. The responses included 2.5, 17, 20, and 25 inches. She decided to interview the students whose answers might have reflected a misunderstanding of proportionality, which she believed the answer of 17 inches indicated. The following is an excerpt from one of those interviews.

Teacher: Can you tell me what you were thinking when you predicted 17 inches as
the answer?

Student: That was easy. I saw that 15 is 9 more than 6, so I need a base that is 9 more than 8.

By interviewing the student, the teacher confirmed her suspicion that the student was thinking additively rather than multiplicatively, so the teacher planned her next lesson with that knowledge in mind. She decided to challenge her students to build similar figures that had different scale factors by using geometric shapes. She instructed her students to record their findings in a table and to make predictions about the enlargement of the sides in relation to the enlargement of the perimeters versus the areas of the similar figures. This was a lesson she had not originally planned to do, but the interviews showed the necessity of giving her students a more concrete investigation to build conceptual understanding.

Probing student thinking: Mathematical discourse

> Discourse entails fundamental issues about knowledge: What makes something true or reasonable in mathematics? How can we figure out whether or not something makes sense? That something is true because the teacher or the book says so is the basis for much traditional classroom discourse. Another view, the one put forth here, centers on mathematical reasoning and evidence as the basis for the discourse. In order for students to develop the ability to formulate problems, to explore, conjecture, and reason logically, to evaluate whether something makes sense, classroom discourse must be founded on mathematical evidence. (NCTM 1991, p. 34)

Student-centered mathematics classrooms promote conversation in small groups, between student and teacher, and between student and student. The conversations about mathematical ideas and work are fundamental to learning. Resnick (1999) suggests that classroom talk that promotes learning must have certain characteristics:

- Students seriously respond to and further develop what others in the group have said.
- Students put forth and demand knowledge that is accurate and relevant to the issue under discussion.
- Students use evidence in ways appropriate to mathematics, including the use of proof.

Students at any age can converse about mathematics. The teacher must develop classroom norms to ensure that important mathematical ideas are discussed at a high level of cognitive demand and that all students participate.

Facilitating effective classroom discourse is not easy. *Professional Standards for Teaching Mathematics* states the following:

> The teacher of mathematics should orchestrate discourse by
>
> - posing questions and tasks that elicit, engage, and challenge each student's thinking;
> - listening carefully to students' ideas;
> - asking students to clarify and justify their ideas orally and in writing;
> - deciding what to pursue in depth from among the ideas that students bring up during a discussion;
> - deciding when and how to attach mathematical notation and language to students' ideas;

- deciding when to provide information, when to clarify an issue, when to model, when to lead, and when to let a student struggle with a difficulty;
- monitoring students' participation in discussions and deciding when and how to encourage each student to participate. (NCTM 1991, p. x)

Teachers and educational researchers have developed many models for classroom discourse. We highlight three in this book, but many others exist.

Accountable talk

According to Resnick (1999, p. 39), "Accountable talk sharpens students' thinking by reinforcing their ability to use knowledge appropriately. As such, it helps develop the skills and habits of mind that constitute intelligence-in-practice."

Accountable talk is conversation in a mathematics classroom that is accountable to community, to accurate knowledge, and to rigorous reasoning. Using accountable talk standards during either whole-class or small-group discussions raises the level of cognitive demand as students' peers challenge them to explain or prove that their thinking is correct.

In an accountable talk session, students discuss a mathematical idea, make conjectures, and support or negate those conjectures mathematically. The conversations are based on a topic and question that you choose to ensure that students meet their learning goals. Accountable talk in a mathematics classroom is best used when students discuss a mathematics problem with other students. Features of accountable talk include the following:

- Restating what another person said
- Restating in different words what someone said
- Expanding on a previously stated idea
- Asking whether an idea, strategy, or solution makes sense
- Asking for clarification when confused
- Using evidence to support statements by (1) including a mathematically accepted definition, (2) using data gathered from an investigation, or (3) negating a conjecture or observation

Teachers direct the discussion by directing students' attention to ideas they want the class to consider, but without judging the worth of the ideas. "Talk moves" include the following:

- Revoicing. *So let me see if I've got your thinking right. You're saying _____?* (Follow with time for students to accept or reject the teacher's formulation.)
- Asking students to restate someone else's reasoning. *Can you repeat what he just said in your own words?*
- Asking students to apply their own reasoning to someone else's reasoning. *Do you agree or disagree, and why?*
- Prompting students for further participation. *Would someone like to add on?*
- Asking students to explicate their reasoning. *Why do you think that?* or *How did you*

arrive at that answer? or *Say more about that.*

- Challenging or offering a counterexample. *Is this always true?* or *Can you think of any examples that would not work?*

As you monitor the discussion, you must also listen for appropriate use of mathematical vocabulary. Teachers who model use of appropriate mathematical vocabulary often find that their students begin to use mathematically correct vocabulary in their discussions, when they make and revise conjectures, and when they pose exceptions and negations to earlier conjectures. Use of accountable talk tends to become more precise as students move through middle school into high school and becomes a powerful step in understanding the nuances of mathematical proof.

Math congress

A math congress is a forum to discuss one or two big ideas that have developed through student work on a specific problem. After students have spent time investigating a problem, they are asked to work with a partner or two to decide what parts of their work they want to share with classmates. Students prepare for the congress by making a chart that shows ideas and strategies that they want to share or discuss.

"The math congress continues the work of helping children become mathematicians in a mathematics community—it is a forum in which children communicate their ideas, solutions, problems, proofs, and conjectures to each other" (Fosnot 2007, p. 39). Fosnot developed the math congress activity to be used as part of a mathematical investigation in a classroom where instruction takes place in a workshop model. She believes that "we become mathematicians by engaging with mathematical problems, finding ways to mathematize them, and defending our thinking in a mathematical community" (Fosnot 2007, p. 27).

The teacher's role in a math congress is complex. Keeping in mind the big idea and the learning goals of the class, you must choose only a few pieces of student work to use and guide the discussion so that each student moves forward in mathematical thinking. Your preparation is essential to a powerful learning experience for the class. Fosnot (2007, p. 29) suggests how the conversation might flow:

- What ideas deserve discussion? In what order?
- Can some of the ideas be generalized? How will you promote this?
- Is there a possible sequence in the discussion that might serve as a scaffold to learning?

You may see that several students have represented their work in similar ways and choose to structure the discussion around the similarities and differences of the representations—and whether they would work for other, but similar, types of problems.

In a different situation, you might decide to choose three different computational strategies, directing discussion toward questions of replicability and efficiency. For example, you could present the following problem to students: *I have $4^1/_2$ yards of ribbon. I want to make bows. For each bow, I need 2 feet of ribbon. How many bows can I make?* Students will probably use many different strategies to solve this problem. You can use the different strategies to explore various meanings of division and division of fractions, to describe the meaning of a remainder, and to work on the big idea that division is the inverse of multiplication.

Fosnot continues, "In addition to helping students learn to calculate with greater understanding and capacity, these methods also allow teachers to capitalize on children's thinking in order to deepen their knowledge of mathematics—a capitalization not available when students are restricted to the traditional method or calculator" (2007, p. 29).

Young Mathematicians at Work: Investigating Decimals, Fractions, and Percents, Grades 4–6, has more suggestions for facilitating a math congress around particular problems.

Using assessment to plan instruction: Neutral feedback

"The most powerful single motivator that enhances achievement is feedback" (Hattie 1992).

Most students, when they get work back, immediately search for a grade. If the grade is good, chances are they will save the paper, but if the grade is average or poor, the papers will probably find their way into the trash bin. Students who receive a grade and written feedback usually look at the grade and often disregard the written feedback. But research is showing that if written comments are the only written information on the page, students read the feedback and seriously consider what it says.

Feedback often falls into two categories: judgmental and informative. If we are to have a positive impact on student achievement, we need less judgmental feedback and more informative feedback. Adapted from Black and Wiliam (1998), table 2.1 illustrates the differences between summative and formative feedback and their impacts on students.

Feedback can be categorized as motivational, evaluative, descriptive, or effective.

Table 2.1—*Continues*

Summative versus formative feedback

Feedback type	Characteristics	Impact on student esteem	Impact on student learning	Student perceptions
Judgmental/ evaluative (summative)	Teacher determines grades; grades come with or without comments	Students who did well feel good about themselves; students who did not do well wonder whether they're smart enough	Surface learning is most likely since the level of cognitive demand is low; students memorize formulas, look for "tricks" and focus on the grade, not their understanding	Mistakes are bad; there must be a math gene; I need to do more memorizing; there are so many tricks to memorize

Table 2.1—*Continued*

Feedback type	Characteristics	Impact on student esteem	Impact on student learning	Student perceptions
Descriptive/ informational (formative)	Teacher responds on the basis of student goals; feedback indicates what needs to be done to reach the goals; praise for what students did well; suggestions for how to improve; praise for trying so hard	All students feel their efforts are recognized, feel they can succeed if they work hard, and "buy in" to the assigned tasks	Deep learning is likely to occur since the level of cognitive demand is high; students advance toward stated learning goals; students display high-quality learning aimed at understanding and improvement	Effort is the key to success; mistakes identify areas that need more effort; learning is fun

Motivational feedback

Motivational feedback is designed to make learners feel that their work is recognized and that they are making progress, as well as to encourage and support learners. Motivational feedback is not designed to give guidance on how to improve the learner's reasoning or to move students forward in the learning process; you can give such guidance on summative assessments.

Evaluative feedback

Evaluative feedback is designed to measure student achievement with a score or a grade and to summarize student achievement—a summative assessment. Evaluative feedback is not designed to give guidance on how to improve the learner's reasoning or to be given on formative assessments, since it is not designed to move students forward in their understanding.

Descriptive feedback

Descriptive feedback is designed to be the following (Wiggins 2005):

- Feedback for learning, a formative assessment
- About the work, not about the student
- Neutral, with nothing in body language, facial expressions, or verbal or written comments to suggest that the student work is erroneous
- Timely
- User-friendly in approach and amount
- Descriptive and specific in regard to performance
- Consistent
- Expert
- Accurate

- Honest, yet constructive
- Derived from concrete standards
- Ongoing

Descriptive feedback is not designed to be a summation of learning; to be about the student, only about the work; or to be judgmental.

Effective feedback

Effective feedback is designed to do the following:

- Move students forward in their understanding
- Support students to internalize the feedback and to use the suggested strategies independently on future work
- Be used by learners to independently move their reasoning to the next level
- Use criterion-based phrases to describe the strengths and weaknesses of learners' work
- Limit feedback to one or two traits or aspects of quality at a time
- Offer an opportunity to "redo" work according to the effective feedback
- Encourage self-reflection

One of the most effective practices for improving student proficiency is to engage students in self-reflection, but students need guidance in this process. Students who regularly receive descriptive or effective feedback are more likely to reflect on their learning progression than are those receiving just grades or a combination of grades with motivational feedback.

Using assessment to plan instruction: Exit cards (exit slips)

How do you know what your students learned in any given mathematics class? Do you know for sure whether your students learned what you think they did? One method of determining whether your students learned what you planned is to use *exit cards*. Exit cards are a quick (no more than five minutes) formative assessment strategy for measuring student learning. Reserve the last few minutes of class time to give students an index card on which they briefly write about what they learned in the lesson or answer one question or perform one computation that you determined beforehand to be a gauge of what you think they should have learned. On the way out the door, students deposit their exit slip into a labeled receptacle.

One teacher uses a general "3–2–1" exit card, and students use index cards to record their responses (fig. 2.10). This teacher begins the next day's lesson by addressing the questions the students had about the prior day's lesson. Sometimes she poses questions for the rest of the class to discuss; other times, she simply raises the question and supplies an answer. This teacher has found that when her students realize that they have to complete the exit card each day, they tend to pay closer attention to the mathematics they are investigating and the problems they are solving. If she forgets to hand out the exit cards, the students remind her. Asked why they would prompt their teacher to ensure that they filled out the exit cards, some students replied, "If I think

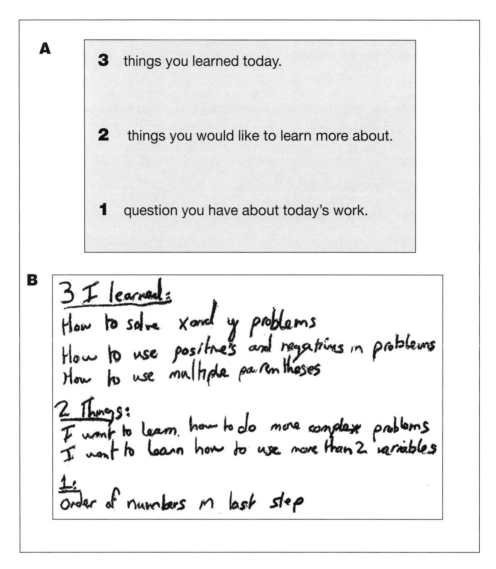

A

3 things you learned today.

2 things you would like to learn more about.

1 question you have about today's work.

B

3 I learned:
How to solve x and y problems
How to use positives and negatives in problems
How to use multiple parentheses

2 Things:
I want to learn how to do more complex problems
I want to learn how to use more than 2 variables

1:
Order of numbers in last step

Fig. 2.10. A 3–2–1 exit card (A) and student responses (B).

and write about what we did in class, it makes it easier to remember and helps me tell my parents what we did in math class." Other students shared that "It makes me realize how hard I worked in math class." Still others responded, "It helps me sort out my thoughts before I have to start thinking about another subject."

These general exit cards can yield information about individual students if you ask them to put their names on the cards. But because the questions are so open, they will not give you evidence that all students have acquired the specific knowledge, understanding, and skill in the mathematics that you had planned for them.

A second teacher uses the exit cards to stay informed about how well her students are maintaining their computational skills. Most of her exit cards are content based. She discovered that her eighth-grade students did not take the work seriously, so she instituted an evaluation system for the cards. Although this grading system is used as a summative assessment, the teacher does use the information to drive her instructional decisions. Together with her students, she developed a rubric for the exit cards (fig. 2.11).

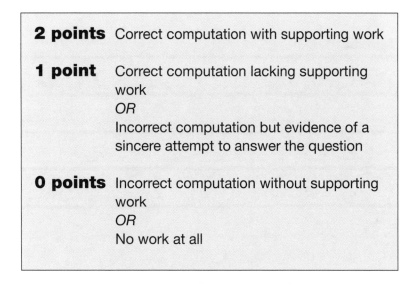

2 points Correct computation with supporting work

1 point Correct computation lacking supporting work
OR
Incorrect computation but evidence of a sincere attempt to answer the question

0 points Incorrect computation without supporting work
OR
No work at all

Fig. 2.11. Grading rubric for students' exit cards

At the end of the week, this teacher adds the total points and uses the grade as a quiz grade. She reports that her students now take the exit card activity seriously. The exit cards add another piece of evidence about her students' proficiencies, and parents are happy to see their children still doing some math to which the parents can relate. But most important, this teacher still uses the student responses to help her prepare the next day's lesson.

A grade 8 student whose teacher asked the students to record the "muddiest point" in the day's lesson completed the following exit card (fig. 2.12):

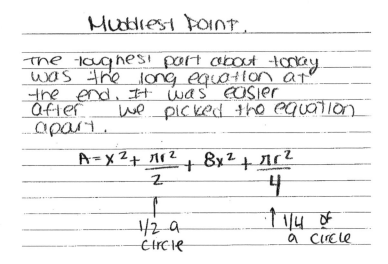

Muddiest Point.

The toughest part about today was the long equation at the end. It was easier after we picked the equation apart.

$$A = x^2 + \frac{\pi r^2}{2} + 8x^2 + \frac{\pi r^2}{4}$$

1/2 a circle   1 1/4 of a circle

Fig. 2.12. An exit card showing material unclear to a student

On the basis of the exit card responses, this teacher planned time for his students to do more problems that incorporated surface area of various figures.

Another teacher asked her students to list the problem with which they had the most difficulty. Many students struggled to determine which was larger: $1/(-9)^8$ or $1/8^9$ (fig. 2.13).

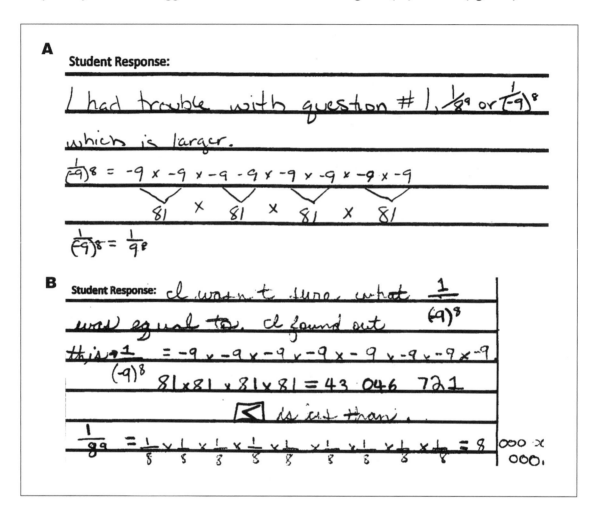

Fig. 2.13. Exit-card responses to a which-is-larger problem

Before instituting exit cards, this teacher would have moved on to the next lesson in her text. After seeing her students' confusion on the exit cards, she decided to spend at least another lesson determining strategies for her students to make comparisons with exponents.

Another teacher asks her students to list what they learned in mathematics class. Figure 2.14 illustrates how differently students in one class can respond.

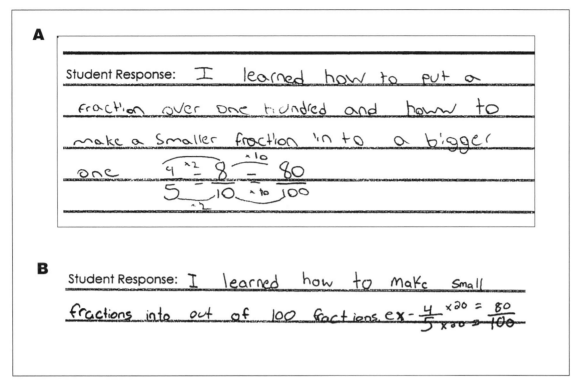

Fig. 2.14. Exit-card responses describing what students learned

Notice the misconception in figure 2.14A. The student believes that finding an equivalent fraction actually changes the value of the original fraction. The student appears to believe that the larger the numbers in a fraction, the greater the value. The work in figure 2.14B illustrates a learned procedure for finding equivalent fractions. This exit card clearly indicates that the student can calculate equivalent fractions procedurally, but exactly what conceptual understanding the student has is unclear. The language "how to make small fractions into out of 100 fractions" lends itself to having an interview with the student.

After examining the exit cards, this teacher decides to assign more problems that include finding equivalent fractions as part of the solution process.

Including exit cards in a lesson benefits both the teacher and the student. Although traditionally exit cards were considered summative assessment, with teachers using them for quiz grades, many teachers use them formatively to plan the next day's lesson. The beauty of using exit cards is that one day's lesson depends on how well the students demonstrated understanding on the previous day. Rather than moving on to the next lesson in the textbook, the flow of daily lessons reflects student understanding from one day to the next. The daily inclusion of these formative assessment strategies and protocols will enable you to use the evidence of your students' learning to give you information for your instructional decisions, help guide your grouping, and assist you in the types of questions you might pose. When the evidence indicates that students do not display a deep level of understanding, it may indicate the need to engage the students in different activities, tasks, and problems.

Selecting tasks or problems for range questions and exit cards is a skill that develops over time. Select range questions to give you a sense of where your students are on the continuum of their learning progression. These tend to be broad questions that tease out how students are thinking, what they recall from past experiences, and how or whether they make connections. Select exit card/slip questions to tease out what your students are bringing away from class that day. These questions are usually more focused than range questions, may relate to procedural skills, and should be selected because of their potential for exposing those understandings or misconceptions that students are walking out of class with.

References

Black, Paul, and Dylan Wiliam. "Assessment and Classroom Learning." *Assessment in Education: Principles, Policy, and Practice* 5 (March 1998): 7–74.

Bright, George W., and Jeane M. Joyner. "Dynamic Classroom Assessment: Linking Mathematical Understanding to Instruction." ETA Cuisenaire. 2005. www.etacuisenaire.com/professionaldevelopment/math/dca/dynamic.jsp (accessed September 9, 2010).

Common Core State Standards Initiative (CCSSI). "The Standards: Mathematics." 2008. www.corestandards.org/the-standards/mathematics (accessed September 10, 2010).

Fosnot, Catherine Twomey. *Young Mathematicians at Work: Investigating Decimals, Fractions, and Percents, Grades 4–6.* Portsmouth, N.H.: Heinemann, 2007.

Hattie, John. "Measuring the Effects of Schooling." *Australian Journal of Education* 36 (April 1992): 5–13.

Heritage, Margaret. "Formative Assessment." Presented at the annual meeting of the Association of State Supervisors of Mathematics in Salt Lake City, April 5, 2008.

Lappan, Glenda, James Fey, William Fitzgerald, Susan Friel, and Elizabeth Phillips. *Growing, Growing, Growing: Exponential Relationships.* Connected Mathematics Project 2. Upper Saddle River, N.J.: Pearson Prentice Hall, 2006.

National Council of Teachers of Mathematics (NCTM). *Professional Standards for Teaching Mathematics.* Reston, Va.: NCTM, 1991.

———. *Principles and Standards for School Mathematics.* Reston, Va.: NCTM, 2000.

———. *Curriculum Focal Points for Prekindergarten through Grade 8 Mathematics: A Quest for Coherence.* Reston, Va.: NCTM, 2006.

Resnick, Lauren B. "Making America Smarter: A Century's Assumptions about Innate Ability Give Way to a Belief in the Power of Effort." *Education Week* 18 (June 1999): 38–40.

Small, Marian, and Amy Lin. *More Good Questions: Great Ways to Differentiate Secondary Mathematics Instruction.* New York: Teachers College Press, 2010.

Wiggins, Grant. "Less Teaching, More Assessing: Learning via Feedback." Presented at the ASCD Conference on Teaching and Learning, San Francisco, 2005.

Chapter 3

Grade 6 Sample Problems Aligned with Curriculum Focal Points

I N ALIGNMENT with the Common Core State Standards mathematical practices, we encourage you to engage your students in making sense of problems and persevering in solving them, reasoning abstractly and quantitatively, constructing viable arguments, modeling with mathematics, using appropriate tools strategically, and attending to precision.

Each problem here will include sample formative assessment strategies taken directly from chapter 2's Toolkit for Formative Assessment.

Problem 1: Rational Numbers

Most students find that working with rational numbers is extremely complicated. Contributing to the difficulties students face is their underlying misconception that a fraction is "a whole number over a whole number" rather than a number or a quantity in its own right. Adding to this confusion is the permeating misconception that the term *multiplication* means "making something bigger."

Problem 1 examines how to make sense of a multistep problem that includes multiple operations and analysis of the results of those computations. Many students demonstrate an ability to manipulate the fractions; however, they struggle to interpret the results of those manipulations. We focus on student thinking in this problem.

> Two groups of tourists each have 60 people. If $3/4$ of the first group and $2/3$ of the second group board buses to go to the museum, how many more people board the first bus than the second bus? Show your work. Explain your reasoning.

Curricular focus

This problem aligns with the following Focal Points, Principles and Standards, and Common Core State Standards.

Focal Points

Number and Operations: Developing an understanding of and fluency with multiplication and division of fractions and decimals. Students multiply and divide fractions and decimals to solve multistep problems.

> ### Principles and Standards
>
> Understand meanings of operations and how they relate to one another. Understand the meaning and effects of arithmetic operations with fractions, decimals, and integers.
>
> ### Common Core State Standards
>
> Make sense of problems and persevere in solving them. Model with mathematics. Attend to precision. Use ratio and rate reasoning to solve real-world and mathematical problems. Apply and extend previous understandings of multiplication and division to divide fractions by fractions.

Assessing prior knowledge

Sample range questions:

a. Is there a difference between $^2/_3 \times 3$ and $^2/_3 \times ^3/_3$? If so, what is the difference? If not, prove that the product is the same.

b. Write a story problem that includes division or multiplication and the numbers $^3/_4$ and 24.

c. Use two different strategies to determine $^3/_5$ of 120.

d. If 27 is $^3/_4$ of a whole, then how might you find $1^1/_4$? Can you do it a second way?

e. If $\bigcirc$ is equivalent to one unit, how might $^2/_3$ be represented? How do you know?

Assessing students at work

Ways to assess students include hinge questions, gallery walks, accountable talk, and observation protocols.

- Pose engaging, clarifying, and refocusing questions as necessary.
- Ask students what factor they have to multiply a fraction by to find an equivalent fraction. This is a good time to reinforce the multiplicative identity and for students to recognize that they are not changing the value of a fraction when they find an equivalent fraction.
- Ask students to support their reasoning.
- Pose "what if?" or "will that always work?" questions.
- Use an observational protocol to record students' investment in the problem, their strategies, their ability to work collaboratively, and their computation.

Linking assessment to instruction

You can use exit cards, gallery walks, interviews, or interventions based on student misconceptions to link assessment to instruction.

> **Sample Exit Cards**
> • List two things you learned about comparing fractions.
> • Which fraction is greater, $^5/_6$ or $^8/_9$? Justify your answer.

Student thinking

Examine the following student work. Think about the conceptual understanding and misconceptions that the students displayed. We have identified sample feedback that might be appropriate for each piece of student work. We start with a positive comment, followed by questions designed to prod students to reflect on their work.

Student A

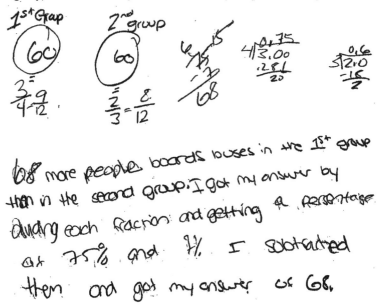

Two groups of tourists each have 60 people. If 3/4 of the first group and 2/3 of the second group board buses to travel to a museum, how many more people in the first group board buses than in the second group? Please show all your work below. Explain your reasoning.

Sample feedback might include the following:

- You found equivalent fractions correctly and efficiently.
- What were you thinking when you subtracted the two decimal values?
- How do the decimal values relate to the number of people boarding the bus?
- Can you explain to me how 68 more people boarded from the first group than the second?
- How can you use the percents you found so accurately to find the number of people boarding the bus?

Student B

> Two groups of tourists each have 60 people. If 3/4 of the first group and 2/3 of the second group board buses to travel to a museum, how many more people in the first group board buses than in the second group? Please show all your work below. Explain your reasoning.

First Group $\frac{3}{4} = \frac{9}{12}$

Second Group $\frac{2}{3} = \frac{8}{12}$

If both groups board the bus the first group will have 1 more person on a bus then the second group. I know this is true because if their are two fractions that have different denominators you find an equivalent fraction for both. So I used 12 as the denominator because 4 and 3 go into 12. So 4 × 3 = 12 and 3 × 3 = 9 so its comes out to $\frac{9}{12}$. Then 3 × 4 = 12 and 2 × 4 = 8 so $\frac{8}{12}$.

Sample feedback might include the following:

- You found equivalent fractions correctly.
- What do the $9/_{12}$ and $8/_{12}$ represent?
- Help me understand how $1/_{12}$ is the same as 1 person.
- How might you use your explanation to answer the question?

Student C

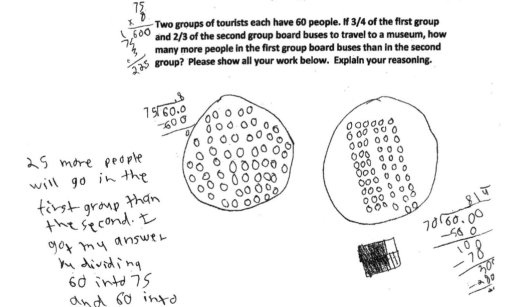

> Two groups of tourists each have 60 people. If 3/4 of the first group and 2/3 of the second group board buses to travel to a museum, how many more people in the first group board buses than in the second group? Please show all your work below. Explain your reasoning.

25 more people will go in the first group than the second. I got my answer by dividing 60 into 75 and 60 into 70 and subtracted the answers.

Sample feedback might include the following:

- *Draw a picture* is a good problem-solving strategy.
- How can you use your picture to check the reasonableness of your answer?
- What other strategy might you use to solve this problem? Would you draw a picture if each group had 300 tourists?
- Can you help me understand why you stated that you were dividing "60 into 75" and "60 into 70"?

Problem 2: Fraction Multiplication and Division

Students need to develop strategies for doing mental mathematics. Problem 2 emphasizes the need for strategic thinking about the relationship between multiplying and dividing fractions and examines student understanding of these concepts. A common misconception is that multiplication always yields a greater numerical product than the quotient found when dividing fractions.

Which computation, $1\frac{2}{3} \times \frac{3}{4}$ or $1\frac{2}{3} \div \frac{3}{4}$, do you predict will result in a greater value? Do not use pen or pencil to compute the answer. Explain your thinking.

Curricular focus

This problem aligns with the following Focal Points, Principles and Standards, and Common Core State Standards.

Focal Points

Number and Operations: Developing an understanding of and fluency with multiplication and division of fractions and decimals.

Principles and Standards

Work flexibly with fractions, decimals, and percents to solve problems.

Common Core State Standards

Reason abstractly and quantitatively. Apply and extend previous understandings of multiplication and division to divide fractions by fractions.

Student thinking

Examine the following student responses to this particular question. Think about the questions you might ask each student. What do you think contributed to these misconceptions? How might you engage these students in determining their own errors? Error analysis assists students in reflecting on their work. What suggestions might you make to students to help them understand their errors?

Student A

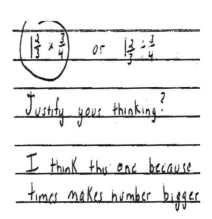

Student A might benefit from being asked to solve a series of multiplication problems that result in a product that is smaller than either factor. Starting with a computation in which both factors are whole numbers might be helpful; then do one in which one factor is zero and the second factor is a whole number. Next, move on to a whole number times a fraction, and finally a fraction times a fraction. The student should model the multiplication each time to engage more senses in the sense-making process of multiplication and then record the factors and the product in an organized list. Paper folding is often helpful.

This student may also benefit from thinking about contextual problems such as *If I had one and two-thirds of a second candy bar and I gave you three-fourths of my candy, how much would you get? Is it possible for you to get more than the one and two-thirds of my candy?* You can model this problem by using a Hershey's chocolate bar if your school allows food.

Student B

Student B shows evidence of understanding that division will yield the number of groups of $3/4$ that are in $1 2/3$, but she does not elaborate on what the product represents. She appears to be thinking about proper fractions as whole numbers rather than as values that are less than one whole.

This student may benefit from modeling both multiplication and division of the same sets of rational numbers until she can articulate what happens when a number is multiplied by a fraction versus what happens when the numbers are divided.

Student C

WITHOUT USING A PEN OR PENCIL TO DO THE MATH, WHICH ANSWER DO YOU PREDICT WILL BE GREATER $1^2/_3 \times ^3/_4$ OR $1\frac{2}{3} \div \frac{3}{4}$

THE ANSWER THAT I PREDICT WILL BE GREATER IS $1\frac{2}{3} \times \frac{3}{4}$ BECAUSE I DID CROSS-MULTIPLICATION IN MY HEAD AND GOT $1^5/_9$ FOR $1\frac{2}{3} \times \frac{3}{4}$ AND $1\frac{1}{2}$ FOR $1\frac{2}{3} \div \frac{3}{4}$ WHICH IS WHY I PREDICT $1\frac{5}{9}$ IS GREATER.

Student C shows why we shouldn't teach an algorithm without allowing students to develop conceptual understanding of the procedure and why it is used and when the algorithm is applicable. The student appears to be confusing the process for solving for an unknown in a proportion with multiplying fractions.

Student D

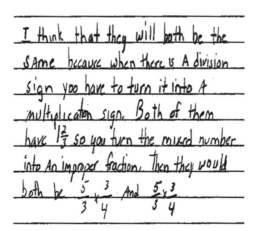

I think that they will both be the same because when there is A division sign you have to turn it into A multiplication sign. Both of them have $1\frac{2}{3}$ so you turn the mixed number into An improper fraction. Then they would both be $\frac{5}{3} \times \frac{3}{4}$ And $\frac{5}{3} \times \frac{3}{4}$

Evidence suggests that student D memorized part of an algorithm, "change the division sign to multiplication," but not the corresponding component, "and invert the divisor." This work and explanation represent the way that many students responded to this problem. This student and others would benefit from modeling multiplication and division of fractions. Folding paper to represent the factors is often helpful in deepening understanding of computation with fractions. Modeling division by using common denominators is often helpful for students who do not understand why we invert and flip the divisor. For example, $1^3/_4 \div {}^3/_4$ can be written as ${}^7/_4 \div {}^3/_4$. Divide numerators and then divide denominators: ${}^7/_4 \div {}^3/_4 = ({}^7/_3)/1$. This equals ${}^7/_3$, or as a mixed number, $2^1/_3$. Challenge the students to prove whether this method will always work.

Problem 3: Multistep Word Problem

Students in grade 6 are accustomed to doing multiple computations and single-step word problems. This situation is unfortunate because the lack of engagement in multistep problems denies them the opportunity to develop problem-solving strategies. This problem is challenging for students since it requires multiple steps and critical thinking at many decision points. Examine the different representations that students used to solve the problem.

After dinner, three friends noticed a bowl of mints on the kitchen counter. Sean took one-third of the mints but returned four because he didn't want to be greedy. Patty then took one-fourth of what was left but returned three for similar reasons. Jimmy then took half of the remainder but threw two green ones back into the bowl. The bowl had only 17 mints left when the raid was over. How many mints were in the bowl to begin with?

Source: Adapted from *Crossing the River with Dogs,* Key Curriculum Press

Curricular focus

This problem aligns with the following Focal Points, Principles and Standards, and Common Core State Standards.

Focal Points

Number and Operations: Developing an understanding of and fluency with multiplication and division of fractions and decimals. Students multiply and divide fractions and decimals to solve problems, including multistep problems.

Principles and Standards

Understand numbers, ways of representing numbers, relationships among numbers, and number systems. Work flexibly with fractions, decimals, and percents to solve problems.

> **Common Core State Standards**
>
> Make sense of problems and persevere in solving them. Model with mathematics.

Assessing prior knowledge

Sample range questions:

a. What problem-solving strategies might you use to solve the following problem? *Half of all the band students stayed up late watching the Super Bowl. Oops, make that half of all the band students and one more. There were 13 tired band students in all the following morning, so how many students were in the band?*

b. Draw a pictorial representation to model $1/2$ of $1/4$ of $1/3$.

c. Which is greater, $2/3$ or $3/4$? (The answer is "of what?" or do both refer to the same-sized whole?)

Assessing students at work

Ways to assess students include hinge questions, gallery walks, accountable talk, and observation protocols.

a. Can you draw a picture or diagram to represent the problem?

b. What other strategy can you use to solve the problem?

c. Do you think you should work with the number of mints removed from the bowl or the number left in the bowl?

d. If you removed $1/3$ but threw back four candies, what fractional part remained in the bowl?

e. If you removed $1/4$ but threw back three mints, what fractional part remained in the bowl?

f. If 27 mints represents $3/4$, how many mints are in $1/4$?

You can also give oral feedback while the students are working on the problem.

Linking assessment to instruction

You can use exit cards, gallery walks, interviews, or interventions based on student misconceptions to link assessment to instruction.

> **Sample Exit Card**
> • List two things you learned in today's class and one thing you still need to practice.

Gallery walk: students record their solutions on large easel paper and post their solutions around the room.

Interview individual students to make their thinking visible.

Student thinking

Examine the following samples of student work for this problem, which were displayed in a gallery walk. What formative assessment strategy might you employ after the work is posted? What feedback might you offer each student?

Student A

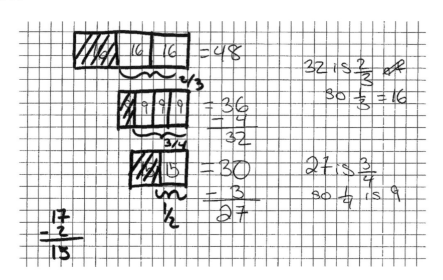

Student A posted a sequence of diagrams accompanied by numerical values. Without labels the diagrams' meaning is unclear. Sample feedback might include the following:

- You have included three interesting diagrams. Help me understand what they represent.

- Since your work doesn't have labels, I am not sure what I am looking at.

- I understand that if 27 is $^3/_4$ as you listed, $^1/_4$ is 9, but without labels I am not sure why you included these in your solution. Please help me follow your thinking.

The teacher decided to interview student A to better understand this student's thinking and what the work represented.

Teacher: Can you explain what the diagram represents?

Student A: When I first did the problem, I got 312 mints but knew that was too big. So I started at the beginning of the problem and drew a picture of the amounts that each person took. The first rectangle is divided into three equal parts, and I shaded in the third that Sean took. The second rectangle shows fourths, but it is only fourths of what was left in the bowl after the third was removed. The next rectangle shows half of what was left after both the third and fourth were removed. So it is not half of the original but half of what was left.

Teacher: After you drew the diagrams, what did you do next?

Student A: I started at the bottom and worked backward. I had to remember to use the part of the mints that were left in the bowl, not the ones taken from the bowl. The 17 mints at the end mean half of what was left plus an additional 2. I had to subtract those 2, for 15 mints in each half, for a total of 30 mints. Then I had to subtract 3 from the mints for 27 mints that represent three-fourths. This means each fourth represents 9 mints, so 36 mints were in the bowl before they took one-fourth. Then I needed to subtract 4 mints that were put back for 32 mints, which represented two-thirds of the mints. If two-thirds is 32, then each third is 16 mints and the beginning number of mints is 48 mints.

Student B

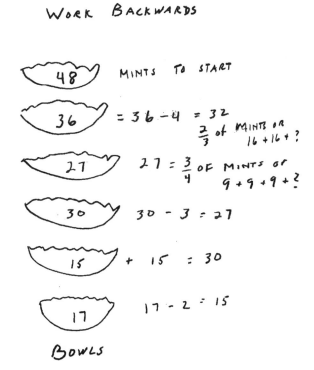

Sample feedback might include the following:

- Your strategy of working backward is effective and efficient.
- Your work is clear and easy to follow, but including labels at every step would help.
- Can you check your solution by working from the answer to the 17 mints left in the bowl?

The teacher decided to interview student B to better understand this student's thinking and what the work represented.

Teacher: Can you explain to me what you were thinking when you solved this problem?

Student B: I was thinking I should work backward with the number of mints left altogether. I made a list of each step that happened.

Teacher: How would you use the list to solve the problem?

Student B: I was thinking that the list would help me organize the information. I started with the number of mints left in the bowl and subtracted to show when more mints were thrown back into the bowl.

Teacher: Did you have any trouble solving the problem?

Student B: Yes, I tried really hard to figure out how I could show one-fourth of 27 since 27 is not divisible by 4.

Teacher: Why were you trying to find one-fourth of 27?

Student B: Because the problem said that Patty took one-fourth of the mints.

Teacher: If Patty took one-fourth, then how much was left?

Student B: Three-fourths—oh, I get it. I was thinking that 27 was one-fourth, not three-fourths, so each fourth would be 9. I have to use what is left, not what is taken out of the bowl.

Student C

LIST

17 - 2 = 15 MINTS

½   15 + 15 = 30 mints

3|4   30 - 3 = 27 MINTS

so ¼ = 9 MINTS

27 + 9 = 36 MINTS

⅔   36 - 4 = 32 MINTS

32 + 16 = 48 MINTS

Sample feedback might include the following:

- You have made a well-organized list.
- I notice that you used fractions to show the fractional part of the mints that were left in the bowl.
- Could you draw a pictorial representation of your list?

The teacher decided to interview student C to better understand this student's thinking and what the work represented.

Teacher: Can you help me understand what you were thinking when you decided to make a list?

Student C: I first read the problem and made a list of the fraction parts that were given: $1/2$, $1/4$, and $1/3$. I tried to solve the problem and came up with 312 mints, which seemed way too many.

Teacher: Did you try to check the reasonableness of your answer, or did you just guess it was too high?

Student C: I just guessed. But when I thought about it more, I figured that if $1/2$ was taken, $1/2$ was left behind. Then if $1/4$ was taken, $3/4$ was left behind, and so if $1/3$ was taken, $2/3$ was left in the bowl. I realized I was working with the wrong part of the fraction.

Teacher: I am not sure what you mean by "working with the wrong part of the fraction."

Student C: Well, I was working with the part that was taken, not the part that was left in the bowl. That makes a big difference, especially when it came to 27 mints. If 27 mints was $1/4$, then $4/4$ would be 108. But if 27 mints was $3/4$, then $4/4$ would be only 36 mints, and that makes more sense to me.

Problem 4: Ratios

Students in grades K–4 focus on thinking additively. By grades 5–6 they are expected to transition to thinking multiplicatively as they begin understand the concept of ratio. They are expected to use ratio language to describe a ratio relationship between two quantities. This problem is designed to evaluate whether students are thinking multiplicatively or additively when working with rates.

A sign in the store window states the following:

12 items for $15
20 items for $23

Which is the better buy? How do you know?

Curricular focus

This problem aligns with the following Focal Points, Principles and Standards, and Common Core State Standards.

Focal Points

Number and Operations: Connecting ratio and rate to multiplication and division. Understanding how to use ratios to find and compare unit rates.

Principles and Standards

Compute fluently and make reasonable estimates. Distinguish multiplicative comparisons from additive comparisons.

Common Core State Standards

Understand ratio concepts and use ratio reasoning to solve problems. Understand the concept of a unit rate a/b associated with a ratio $a{:}b$ with $b \neq 0$ and use rate language in the context of a ratio relationship.

Assessing prior knowledge

Sample range questions:

a. Turn to a partner and explain what the term *per* means.

b. If you had to compare the two ratios 5/9 and 3/7, what strategies might you use to determine which ratio is the largest if you cannot convert them into decimal form or use a calculator?

c. Signs on the shelf at the local supermarket show the following information: *$4.5623 per unit $0.3214 per unit $0.5823 per unit.* Turn to a partner and discuss what the signs mean.

d. What does the term *rate* mean?

e. What does a ratio represent?

Assessing students at work

Ways to assess students include hinge questions, gallery walks, accountable talk, and observation protocols.

A pivotal concept necessary for solving this problem is that ratios are multiplicative, not additive. Examine the following student work. Think about hinge questions that might have been appropriate to ask given the evidence in each student's work. Recall that hinge questions are asked while students are working.

When you are listening to students while they are at work solving a problem, presenting their work, or examining their written work, determining whether students are "communicating a misunderstanding or miscommunicating an understanding" is crucial (Bright and Joyner 2005). Differentiating between communicating a misunderstanding or miscommunicating an understanding is also important. As you examine the following student work, focus on which pieces of work show evidence of communicating conceptual and procedural understanding and which pieces of student work display evidence of communicating either conceptual or procedural misunderstanding.

Student A

Problem:

A sign in the store window states:

o 12 items for $15

o 20 items for $23

o Which is the best buy? How do you know?

There the same because you have 12 for 15 and 12 for 23 each one you spend 3 extra dollars there is no better deal.

Evidence supports that student A misunderstands the concept. The evidence that supports the fact that this student is thinking additively rather than multiplicatively is visible when he subtracted 15 – 12 for a difference of 3 and 23 – 20 for a similar difference of 3. The student makes no attempt to identify or find the unit rate for each ratio but instead relies on the difference between the number of items and the cost for that quantity of items. This student would benefit from building a ratio table for the costs of various items followed by a comparison of the costs of the same number of items. This visual representation illustrates an efficient and accurate manner of comparing the rates:

Number of Items	12	24	36	48	60
Cost of Items	$15	$30	$45	$60	$75

Number of Items	20	40	60	80	100
Cost of Items	$23	$46	$69	$92	$115

Student B

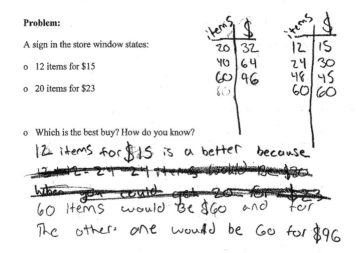

Problem:

A sign in the store window states:

o   12 items for $15

o   20 items for $23

o   Which is the best buy? How do you know?

12 items for $15 is a better because ~~12 12=24 24 items would be $36~~ ~~when you could get 36 for $23~~ 60 items would be $60 and for The other one would be 60 for $96

Student B set up rate tables. This student made some procedural errors such as reversing $23 as $32, which accounts for the mistaken conclusion. The student shows evidence of thinking multiplicatively and recognizes the value of a rate table. This student is miscommunicating an understanding. Making a graphical representation for the data in the table may help this student. The rate of change is constant, so the graph should be linear. If any points reside outside the line, the student should be encouraged to reexamine the computation. Using a graph to represent data in a table is an important skill for students to develop.

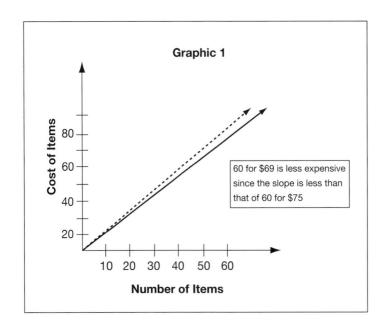

Graphic 1

60 for $69 is less expensive since the slope is less than that of 60 for $75

Student C

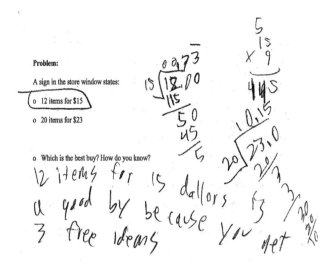

Student C confused the divisor and dividend in one division example and showed computational errors in dividing $23 by 20. These errors convey the student's procedural misunderstanding and omission of checking the reasonableness of the answer. Twenty-three dollars divided by 20 cannot come close to being $10.15. The division is not consistent, offering evidence that this student would benefit from an intervention that would address these procedural misunderstandings. This student may do well by using a multiplication menu for division:

For $15 ÷ 12:
1 group of 12 = 12
2 groups of 12 = 24
1/2 group of 12 = 6
1/4 group of 12 = 3
So 1 group of 12 + 1/4 group of 12 = 15, so the unit price is 11/4, or $1.25

For $23 ÷ 20:
1 group of 20 = 20
2 groups of 20 = 40 (too large)
1/2 group of 20 = 10 (too large)
1/4 group of 20 = 5 (too large)
1/5 group of 20 = 4 (too large)
1/10 group of 20 = 2
1/20 group of 20 = 1

So 1 group of 20 + 1/10 group of 20 + 1/20 group of 20 equals 23, or a unit price of $1 + 3/20, or $1.15.

The multiplication menu is not the most efficient method for solving this problem, but it might clarify the meaning of division and how division relates to multiplication. Interviewing this student would be helpful.

Student D

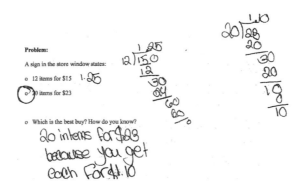

Student D understands the basic procedure for doing long division; however, in the second example she neglected to add additional zeros, resulting in an incorrect computation. The student appears to be thinking multiplicatively.

Linking assessment to instruction

You can use exit cards, gallery walks, interviews, or interventions based on student misconceptions to link assessment to instruction. As teachers, we have to reflect on the student responses that present themselves at any time. The following is a suggested list of questions to ponder as you work with your students:

- What hinge questions might you ask students that may help them develop a conceptual understanding of the concepts that have eluded them so far? Are you asking refocusing, engaging, or clarifying questions when you are posing questions to move your students' thinking in another direction?

- Are the computational errors as important in this context as the conceptual misunderstandings?

- Since we want students to compute accurately, what hinge questions might you ask to guide those students who struggled with computation to more accurate answers?

- What is your next-step lesson or intervention to move those students who are thinking additively toward thinking multiplicatively? What activities might help these students think multiplicatively?

- What is your next-step lesson or extension to deepen understanding for those students who understood the concept and demonstrated procedural accuracy? If the students drew a table, might you suggest that they graph the relationship for each rate?

Problem 5: Spatial Reasoning

Problem 5 requires students to make various decisions relating to spatial reasoning. Students who have little experience modeling situations often struggle when it becomes a necessary component in problem solving. This problem also indicates the importance of consistently using and expecting accountable talk both orally and in writing.

> The Smiths are going to build a new one-story house. The floor of the house will be rectangular, with a length of 30 feet and a width of 20 feet. The house will have a living room, a kitchen, two bedrooms, and a bathroom. The bathroom will have an area of 50 square feet.
> - In part (a) below, create a floor plan.
> - In part (b) below, create a table to record each room's dimensions and the total number of square feet for each room.
>
> *Source:* Adapted from Strait Regional School Board 2009, Nova Scotia, Canada

Curricular focus

This problem aligns with the following Focal Points, Principles and Standards, and Common Core State Standards.

Focal Points

Measurement and Geometry: Problems that involve areas and volumes, calling on students to find areas or volumes from lengths or to find lengths from volumes or areas and lengths, are especially appropriate. Understanding how to use ratios to find and compare unit rates.

Principles and Standards

Draw geometric objects with specified properties, such as side lengths or angle measures. Select and apply techniques and tools to accurately find length, area . . . to appropriate levels of precision.

Common Core State Standards

Solve real-world and mathematical problems involving area, surface area, and volume.

Assessing prior knowledge

Sample range questions:

    a.   What is the difference between feet and square feet?

    b.   How many dimensions make up the area of a room?

    c.   What comes into your mind when you hear the word *dimension*?

    d.   Think about and record everything you know about the area of a room. Discuss your information with a partner.

    e.   About how many square feet are in a square yard?

    f.   About how many square inches are in a square foot?

If students struggle with range questions about the relationship between square feet and square yards, try the following instructional intervention: Students use chalk or shoe polish, a ruler, or a yardstick to model the relationship between feet and yards, and square feet and square yards, either on the floor or on the playground. Instruct them to measure out a length of 1 yard and a width of 1 yard. They complete the square yard. Next, they measure out as many square feet as possible within that square yard. You can also encourage them to draw as many square inches as possible into 1 square foot to see the relationship among square inches, square feet, and square yards. This activity will give the students a visual representation of square feet and square yards.

Assessing students at work

Ways to assess students include hinge questions, gallery walks, accountable talk, and observation protocols.

- Initiate a gallery walk for vocabulary terms: *length*, *width*, *area*, *perimeter*, *square feet*, *square yard*, and *perimeter.*

- Listen for accountable talk, which should include appropriate reference to feet, square feet, yard, square yard, area, and dimensions.

- Encourage students to correctly use mathematical language for dimensions (feet or yards) and area (square feet or square yards).

- Play a round of *I have? Who has?* with geometric terms.

Student thinking

Examine the following examples of student work.

- What are the conceptual misunderstandings?

- What are the procedural misunderstandings?

- What questions would you ask each student about the work?

- If you decided to interview each student, what misconceptions might you focus your conversation on?

Student A

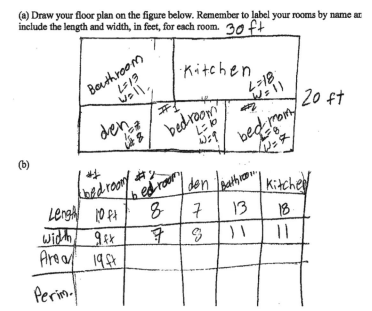

(a) Draw your floor plan on the figure below. Remember to label your rooms by name and include the length and width, in feet, for each room.

Student A appears to be confusing area and perimeter, as the table indicates. Also, in the diagram the widths do not add up to the 20 feet indicated on the outside of the diagram, nor does the length sum to 30 feet. This student may benefit from being asked to create diagrams for other situations—for example, design a playground to certain specifications, or design a dream yard to include a play area, a pool, a patio, and a grassy area given certain overall specifications.

Student B

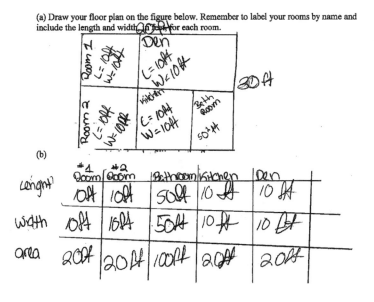

(a) Draw your floor plan on the figure below. Remember to label your rooms by name and include the length and width, in feet, for each room.

Student B has labeled the dimensions of length and width correctly; however, the dimensions in the rooms do not match the given dimensions. The student has inappropriately labeled the 50-square-foot area for the bathroom and has not shown evidence of how the dimensions of the room relate to the dimensions of the floor plan. The student also demonstrates a misconception about how to find area and what the appropriate label for area is.

Student C

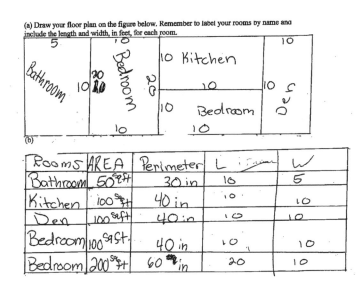

Student C also demonstrates misconceptions in completing a diagram to given specifications. Although the bathroom measurements meet the criteria of an area of 50 square feet, one wall is labeled 10 feet for the bathroom but 20 feet for the bedroom. The student appropriately labeled the area of each room with square feet but reverted to inches for the dimensions. This student may need more experience making scale drawings.

Linking assessment to instruction

You can use exit cards, gallery walks, interviews, or interventions based on student misconceptions to link assessment to instruction.

Sample Exit Cards

- If a room has an area of 160 square feet and one dimension is 16 feet, how might you find the length of the second dimension?
- How might you find the number of square inches in a square yard?
- What information does the perimeter give?
- What information does the area offer?

Problem 6: Area and Perimeter

Evidence from the 1994 Third International Mathematics and Science Study illustrated the difficulty that U.S. students have with multistep area and perimeter problems. By sharing student work, we are drawing attention to many common student misconceptions about working from the area to find perimeter.

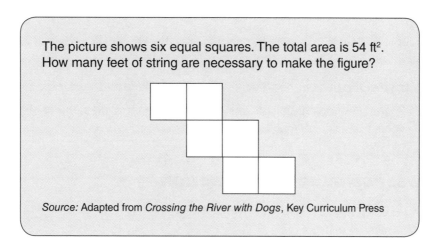

The picture shows six equal squares. The total area is 54 ft². How many feet of string are necessary to make the figure?

Source: Adapted from *Crossing the River with Dogs*, Key Curriculum Press

Curricular focus

This problem aligns with the following Focal Points, Principles and Standards, and Common Core State Standards.

Focal Points

Measurement and Geometry: Problems that involve areas and volumes, calling on students to find areas of volumes from lengths or to find lengths from volumes or areas and lengths, are especially appropriate.

Principles and Standards

Apply appropriate techniques, tools, and formulas to determine measurements.

Common Core State Standards

Find the area of right triangles, other triangles, special quadrilaterals, and polygons by composing into rectangles or decomposing into triangles and other shapes; apply these techniques in the context of solving real-world and mathematical problems.

Assessing prior knowledge

Sample range questions:

a. Turn to a friend and discuss how the area of a figure is the same as or different from the perimeter of that same figure.

b. What information does the area reveal?

c. What information does the perimeter give?

Assessing students at work

Ways to assess students include hinge questions, gallery walks, accountable talk, and observation protocols.

- Listen for accountable talk, which should include the appropriate labels for area and perimeter.
- Ask clarifying questions if the students neglect to include all sides of the squares.
- Ask clarifying questions if the students are double counting the number of sides rather than making allowance for the shared sides.

Linking assessment to instruction

You can use exit cards, gallery walks, interviews, or interventions based on student misconceptions to link assessment to instruction.

Gallery walk: List the following terms on easel paper and post around the room. Pair students or allow them to work in small groups to define *perimeter*, *area*, *volume*, *length*, *width*, and *line segment*. Have them also list the formulas for area of parallelograms, triangles, and circles.

Student thinking

Examine the following examples of student work.

Student A

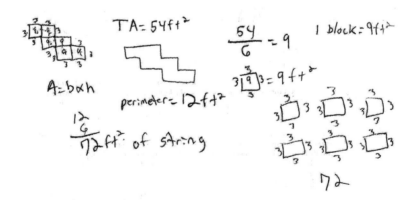

Student A understands how to determine the length of a square given its area. The student also labeled all components of the work but erroneously labeled the length of string as square feet. This student displays the difficulty of not accounting for the shared side lengths between squares. This student may have benefited from a conversation while she was solving the problem and by being asked to model the problem with tiles to determine whether she would see the shared sides more clearly. This student might benefit from solving pattern problems that include shared sides.

Student B

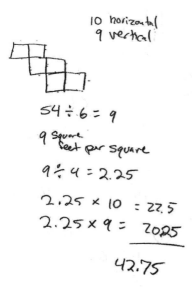

Student B correctly accounts for all the lines on all the figures but neglects to label his computational work. He appears to have taken the total area and divided it by the six visible squares to find an area for each square to be 9 square units. The student appears to have confused area with perimeter and divided by 4 sides to get a length of 2.25 units.

Student C

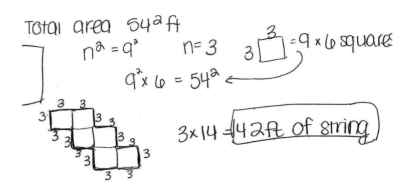

Student C appropriately found the length of each square to be 3. But the student did not label this value and uses the exponential notation for square feet incorrectly. The student neglected to count the sides of the squares on the inside. He may have just assumed that he needed the perimeter, but the problem did not state that. We think that a conversation with this student will clarify any misunderstandings.

The nonroutine problems dealing with area and perimeter caused students a great deal of difficulty, yet when we spoke to the students whose work we show here, each could recite the formulas for area and perimeter.

REFERENCE

Bright, George W., and Jeane M. Joyner. "Dynamic Classroom Assessment: Linking Mathematical Understanding to Instruction." ETA Cuisenaire. 2005. www.etacuisenaire.com/professionaldevelopment/math/dca/dynamic.jsp (accessed September 9, 2010).

Chapter 4

Grade 7 Sample Problems Aligned with Curriculum Focal Points

I N ALIGNMENT with the Common Core State Standards mathematical practices, we encourage you to engage your students in making sense of problems and persevering in solving them, reasoning abstractly and quantitatively, constructing viable arguments, modeling with mathematics, using appropriate tools strategically, and attending to precision.

This chapter offers samples of effective classroom practices driven by the challenges and misconceptions articulated in sample student work. The approaches we include are gallery walks, preassessment strategies, strategies for assessing students at work, exit card sample questions, and teaching strategies designed to clarify student thinking and develop understanding.

Problem 1: Proportional Relationships and Remainders

We include the following problem to show the importance of helping students recognize the proportional relationship between their answer and the original givens in the problem, not to compute answers. We include student work that highlights the various strategies students use to solve it. The student work also illustrates the challenges students face in making sense of remainders in contextual situations. We focus on student thinking and reasoning in this problem.

A certain machine produces 300 nails per minute. At this rate, how long will it take the machine to produce enough nails to fill 5 boxes of nails if each box will contain 250 nails?

Source: National Assessment of Educational Progress (NAEP)–released item

Curricular focus

This problem aligns with the following Focal Points, Principles and Standards, and Common Core State Standards.

Focal Points

Number and Operations and Algebra and Geometry: Developing an understanding of and applying proportionality, including similarity. Students extend their work with ratios to develop an understanding of proportionality that they apply to solve single- and multistep problems in many contexts.

Principles and Standards

Understand and use ratios and proportions to represent quantitative relationships.

Common Core State Standards

Model with mathematics. Analyze proportional relationships and use them to solve real-world and mathematical problems. Recognize and represent proportional relationships between quantities.

Assessing prior knowledge

Sample range questions:

a. Fill in the missing values.

Input	Output
3	5
8	15
	21
21	

b. If Jaime can bicycle an average of 13 miles per hour, how long will it take him to pedal 6 miles?

c. If you know the average rate of speed a bird flies and how long it takes the bird to fly a certain distance, how can you determine how far the bird flew?

d. If you know the average rate and distance, how might you find the time it takes to cover that distance?

Assessing students at work

Ways to assess students include hinge questions, gallery walks, accountable talk, and observation protocols.

Listen for accountable talk. Encourage students to include appropriate mathematical language that uses the terms *rate* and *per*.

Student thinking

For each of the following students we suggest appropriate questions or strategies that may help them make better sense of the problem and/or how to represent the data given.

Student A

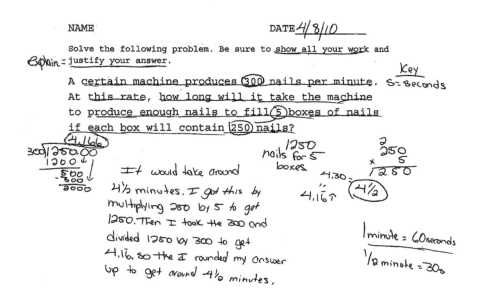

Student A demonstrates a computational approach to solving the problem. All the values are labeled and the student included a legend for seconds. A consideration when probing the student's thinking is to ask the student to explain rounding 4.166 to $4^1/_2$ minutes. No evidence exists to explain whether the student rounded 4.166 to 4.2 and assumed that ".2" meant half a minute or if the leap to $4^1/_2$ was due to a comfort level with the fact that half a minute is 30 seconds. The only way to determine exactly what the student is thinking is to converse with the student, either in an interview or while the student is working on the problem.

Student B

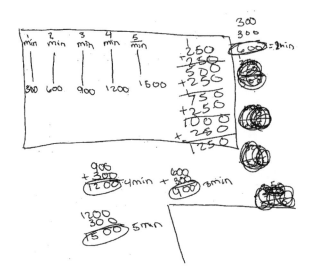

Student B chose to represent the problem situation with a ratio table. The work shows evidence that the student recognizes the ratio between minutes and number of nails, but the answer to the question is missing. The student illustrates that 1200 nails can be packaged in 4 minutes and 1500 nails in 5 minutes but does not address the time that packaging 1250 nails takes. Highlighting the student's use of ratio (the compound unit [1 minute/300 nails] and helping her understand that she can deconstruct this larger unit into smaller units that keep the same relationship) might be helpful. For example, if producing 300 nails takes 1 minute, how many nails could be made in half a minute? This student will also benefit from being prodded to think about the relationship between 250 and 300. For example, a different kind of question would be "How long would it take to make 100 nails, 50 nails, etc.?"

Student C

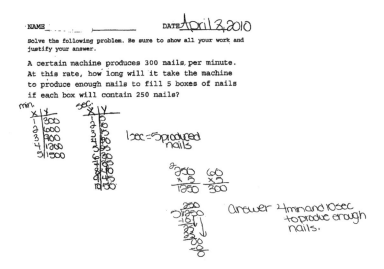

Student C models the problem with two input–output tables and demonstrates an understanding of the problem. The first table is partly labeled, indicating that the input is minutes, and we are left to assume that the output is nails. The second input table indicates the number of nails produced in seconds. Although the student's own words do not explain, one can understand from the student's seconds table that in 10 seconds, 50 nails are produced. The student appears to have taken the fact that in 4 minutes 1200 nails were produced from the minutes table and combined that with the 10 seconds it takes to produce 50 nails for the answer of 4 minutes, 10 seconds. This student may benefit from being asked to justify the answer. This student as well as the whole class might benefit from this student's presenting the solution together with an oral explanation. It's interesting that this child couldn't solve the problem with one table. It is also interesting that the x and y change meanings from one chart to the other. We cannot know whether the child realizes that to get from 60 seconds to 1 second, a constant relation between $60/300 = {}^1/_5$ and 1 second for every 5 nails must be maintained.

Student D

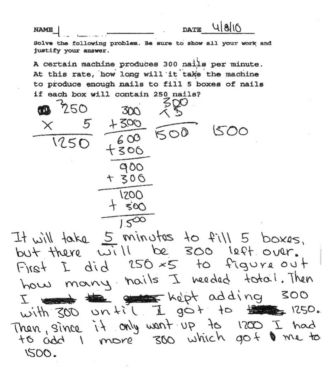

This student is not thinking multiplicatively, but additively, and therefore cannot use the proportional relationship to reason with between the number of nails and the time. The student relies on addition and multiplication and appears to be challenged with a number of nails that is not a multiple of 300. This student correctly states how long packaging 1200 nails and 1500 nails will take but does not answer the query about 1250 nails. Using a ratio table might help this student, as would working with what is known (e.g., that a machine makes 300 nails in 1 minute) to help him think about what is unknown (how long producing five boxes with 250 nails in each box takes).

Tell the child, "I'm going to set this up on a table with the important information," and then build the table with him. Questions you might ask include the following: *So if we know 2 minutes is 600 nails, could we figure out what 4 minutes would be?* (You double the time, you double the nails.) *What about 8 minutes?* Then to start working the other way, *What about half a minute? What about if we wanted to put only 100 nails in the box? 50? 250?* The goal of the intervention here is to help the child have a tool to use to begin to reason proportionally. The following is a sample tool:

Time	1	?			
Nails	300	250			

Time	1	2	4	8	
Nails	300	600	1200	2400	

Time	1	$\frac{1}{2}$	$\frac{1}{4}$	?	
Nails	300	150	60	100	

Linking assessment to instruction

You can use exit cards, gallery walks, interviews, or interventions based on student misconceptions to link assessment to instruction.

Sample Exit Cards

- If a hospital supply company sells pill-dispensing cups at a rate of 1000 cups for $0.25, how much would they charge for a single cup if it were possible to do so? Explain how you know.
- The I Saw Lumber company sells nuts and bolts. If they sell 250 nuts at a cost of $27.50, what is the cost per nut? Explain your reasoning.
- The Kennedy Middle School store sells packages of stickers. If they charge 57 cents per package for a total of $22.23, how many packages of stickers did they sell? Justify your answer.

Problem 2: Paying Interest

In this problem we are emphasizing pre- and postassessments and offering a classroom activity to address the student misconceptions in the main problem. How well the students demonstrate understanding on the range question may indicate their confidence in solving the problem.

Joe bought a video game player for $276.00 at Eli's Electronics in December. Later that month, he paid $40.00 toward his bill. If the store charges 2.8% per month interest on the unpaid portion of his bill, how much interest will Joe have to pay in January?

Curricular focus

This problem aligns with the following Focal Points, Principles and Standards, and Common Core State Standards.

Focal Points

Number and Operations and Algebra and Geometry: Use ratio and proportionality to solve a wide variety of percent problems, including problems involving discounts, interest, taxes, tips, and percent increase or decrease.

Principles and Standards

Work flexibly with fractions, decimals, and percents to solve problems.

Common Core State Standards

Reason abstractly and quantitatively. Apply and extend previous understandings of operations with fractions to add, subtract, multiply, and divide rational numbers. Convert a rational number to a decimal by using long division.

Assessing prior knowledge

Sample range questions:

a. Turn to a partner and explain what the term *percent* means.

b. If you shade in $3/8$ of this 10-by-10 rectangle, how many squares will be shaded? Justify your response.

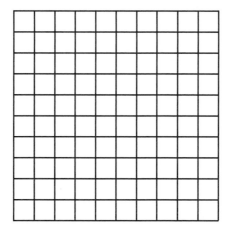

c. Say your dad earned a salary of $50,000, but his boss must cut everyone's salary by 10%. To make up for the loss in pay, your dad's boss tells him he will get a 10% raise the following year so he will not be losing any money. Is this a good deal for your dad? If so, why? If not, why not?

Assessing students at work

Ways to assess students include hinge questions, gallery walks, accountable talk, and observation protocols. Sample hinge questions may include the following:

a. Predict how much interest you would expect to pay on $236 at a rate of 2.8% per year. Do you expect the interest to be a large amount or a small amount? Tell me how you know.

b. If you continue to pay $40 per month on the balance of the bill, how might you determine when you will finish paying off your debt?

Listen for accountable talk. Students should be encouraged to use appropriate mathematical language to include the following:

- Describing the percent interest as 2.8% (two and eight-tenths percent)
- Down payment of $40
- Remaining balance

Student thinking

For each of the following students we suggest appropriate questions or strategies that may help them make better sense of the problem and/or how to represent the data given.

Student A

1. Joe bought a video game player for $276.00 at Eli's Electronics in December. In January, he paid $40.00 toward his bill. If the store charges 2.8% per month interest on the unpaid portion of his bill, how much interest will Joe have to pay in January?

$276 - 40 = 236.00$

$236.00 + 6.60 = 242.60$

236.00×0.28

$\$242.60$ is the interest.

Student A correctly shows all the correct steps when solving the problem. The student remembered to subtract the down payment, calculated the interest correctly, and added the interest to the balance—but mislabeled the final answer. This student may benefit from a conversation about the realism that someone would pay more than the balance for the item in interest or a conversation that focuses on the reasonableness of an answer.

Student B

1. Joe bought a video game player for $276.00 at Eli's Electronics in December. In January, he paid $40.00 toward his bill. If the store charges 2.8% per month interest on the unpaid portion of his bill, how much interest will Joe have to pay in January?

$$0.28\% = 0.28$$

$$
\begin{array}{r}
278.00 \\
\times\ .028 \\
\hline
227900 \\
550000 \\
+0000000 \\
\hline
07.72900
\end{array}
$$

$$
\begin{array}{r}
\$40.00 \\
+\ 7.78 \\
\hline
\$47.78
\end{array}
$$

Student B correctly converted the interest rate into a decimal but erred with placement of the decimal point. That error notwithstanding, the student demonstrated accuracy with the procedure for multiplication with decimals. However, the student appears to be confused about the $40 and what it represents and on which value to calculate the interest. The computation appears to be accurate although misguided. An interview with this student would most likely be beneficial to discover why the student added the interest to the down payment.

Student C

1. Joe bought a video game player for $276.00 at Eli's Electronics in December. In January, he paid $40.00 toward his bill. If the store charges 2.8% per month interest on the unpaid portion of his bill, how much interest will Joe have to pay in January?

Cost for
Item →

40 dollars paid

$$
\begin{array}{r}
6\ 16 \\
278.00 \\
-\ 40.00 \\
\hline
\$\ 236.00
\end{array}
$$

price after 40$ subtract
2.8% Interest

$$
\begin{array}{r}
2\ 4 \\
236 \\
\times\ .28 \\
\hline
18\ 88 \\
4\ 72\ 0 \\
\hline
\$\ 66.08
\end{array}
$$

Joe will have to pay 66.08 towards his bill in January

Interest for January

Student C labeled all work clearly and demonstrates an understanding of the down payment and what to do with a rate of interest. But the work communicates a misconception on how to convert a mixed-number rate to a decimal. Despite his computational prowess, this student may benefit from engaging in meaningful practice converting percents to decimals but, more important, needs to be engaged in thinking about the logic of the answer. Discussion with the child about the appropriate use of benchmark percents and their decimal equivalents as reasoning tools would be beneficial. For instance, *If 10% of $236 is $23.60, is it possible that 2.8% of $236 is more?* Another way to help this student might be to use landmark percents and decimal equivalents to help him understand why 2.8% could not be 0.28. For example, *How would you write 25% as a decimal? 50%? 10%? 20%? 5%? 1%?* The student may also benefit from using money as a context for understanding.

Linking assessment to instruction

You can use exit cards, gallery walks, interviews, or interventions based on student misconceptions to link assessment to instruction.

Instructional activity: Instruct as many students as will fit at the board at one time to go to the board and draw a large *T*. Students who work at their seats (they may use individual whiteboards or paper) do the same. Instruct students to record a dictated list of percents on the left side of the *T*. Instruct the students to write the corresponding decimal values on the right side. See the following examples:

%	Decimal		%	Decimal
10			10	0.10
6			6	0.06
1.6			1.6	0.016
3			3	0.03
1.5			1.5	0.015

After students complete the table, either the teacher or a student reads out the correct decimal values. Students erase the dictated values and replace them with another list of rates. As students work, the teacher's role is to observe and intervene with any students who may demonstrate uncertainty or incorrect decimal values before those misconceptions solidify. After a short interval, dictate a list of decimal values and challenge the students to find the percents (Collins and Dacey 2010a).

Gallery walk: Post easel paper with the terms *down payment*, *balance*, *debt*, *interest*, and *compounded interest* around the room and ask students to work in small groups to list what they think each term means. One member from each group records the definition of each term on the easel paper. Gallery walks offer a safe environment for students since the activity lists a group understanding, not an individual student's thinking.

Sample Exit Cards

- Show two different ways to find 35% of 120.
- If the cost of a video game increases $9.00 from its original price of $39.00, what is the percent increase?
- Jorge left some numbers off the number line below. Fill in the numbers that should go in A, B, and C.

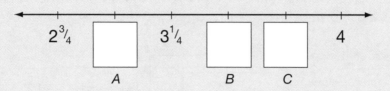

Source: Adapted from NAEP-released item

One teacher often uses exit cards to review concepts that her students had a hard time with. She thought all her students would find the question about the mixed numbers too easy. She was surprised to see one student's misconception:

1. Jorge left some numbers off the number line below. Fill in the numbers that should go in *A*, *B*, and *C*.

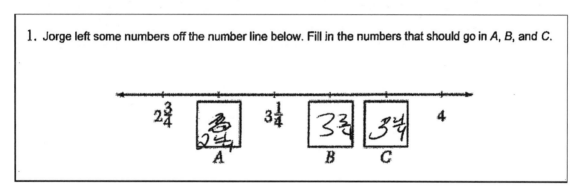

The work gives some evidence to support the student understanding that there is an increment of $1/4$, even though the student did not uniformly apply this reasoning. The inclusion of both $2^4/_4$ and $3^4/_4$ raised concern about the student's understanding of how to represent the value of 1. She also wondered what the student might record if a second blank space existed between $2^3/_4$ and $3^1/_4$. She also pondered what the student might include in a number line that simply recorded the $2^3/_4$ and the 4. Since this appeared to be an isolated case, she decided to interview the student and individualize later activities. One activity she plans to include is asking the student to count by using fractional intervals. Another will include an open number line on which students will be instructed to label all values.

Problem 3: Surface Area

Geometry and measurement continue to challenge middle school students. We include this surface area problem to highlight how easily you can pose challenging area problems that interest students. This problem emphasizes feedback. We give sample comments that could be instrumental in deepening student understanding.

Ray had a block of wood in the shape of a rectangular prism. The block and its dimensions are shown below:

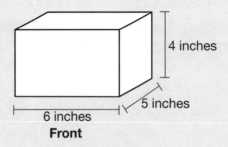

Front

a. Ray painted the front face of the block red. What is the area of the face he painted red? Show or explain how you got your answer.
b. Ray painted the top and bottom faces of the block black. What is the area of the faces he painted black? Show or explain how you got your answer.
c. Ray painted the other faces of the block white. What is the area of the faces he painted white? Show or explain how you got your answer.

Source: Massachusetts Department of Elementary and Secondary Education. Grade 7 Mathematics. Massachusetts Comprehensive Assessment System–Released Items Document, 2008–2009

Curricular focus

This problem aligns with the following Focal Points, Principles and Standards, and Common Core State Standards.

Focal Points

Measurement and Geometry and Algebra: Developing an understanding of and using formulas to determine surface areas and volumes of three-dimensional shapes. By decomposing two- and three-dimensional shapes into smaller, component shapes, students find surface areas and develop and justify formulas for the surface areas and volumes of prisms and cylinders.

> ### Principles and Standards
>
> Develop strategies to determine the surface area and volume of selected prisms, pyramids, and cylinders.
>
> ### Common Core State Standards
>
> Solve real-life and mathematical problems involving area, volume, and surface area of two- and three-dimensional objects composed of triangles, quadrilaterals, polygons, cubes, and right prisms.

Assessing prior knowledge

Sample range questions:

a. Hold an empty paper towel or toilet paper tube up for all students to see. Challenge them to explain what strategies they might use to find an approximate surface area of the tube. After a short period, record the students' strategies on the board. Follow up by asking the students to predict the surface area by using one of the strategies. Listen specifically for students to include phrases such as "I know a paper towel roll is a little taller than a rolled-up sheet of paper" or "I know if I cut the paper towel roll and unravel it I will get a rectangle, and I know how to find the area of a rectangle."

b. Give the students graph paper and ask them to predict how many two-dimensional nets they can make that will fold up into a closed cube with no overlapping faces. Demonstrate one example, such as the following:

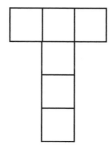

(There are ten additional ways of constructing a net for a cube.) Instruct them to find the surface area of the nets.

Assessing students at work

Ways to assess students include hinge questions, gallery walks, accountable talk, and observation protocols.

Since many students confuse linear measurement with spatial measurement, you must listen to your students to determine whether they are using accountable talk. Students should demonstrate an understanding that inches are one-dimensional and square inches are two-dimensional and use the correct vocabulary in their group discussions. They must also recognize and state that area is two-dimensional, and therefore the unit label they should use is "square inches." One classroom teacher reports that she models accountable talk, and her students adopt the appropriate terminology as a result. She is particularly fond of this method of reinforcing appropriate language since it does not embarrass students or call undue attention to the incorrect terminology but rather subtly emphasizes the correct language. For example:

Emma: I found the area by multiplying 6 inches by 4 inches to get an area of 24 inches.

Teacher: When you found the area by multiplying the length by the width, your area was 24 square inches.

Emma: Yes, and when I found the area of the side face, I multiplied 5 inches by 4 inches and got an area of 20 square inches.

Each time an opportunity arises for the teacher to interject the correct unit description, she does so; she reports that her students do adopt the correct terms as a result.

Student thinking

For each of the following students we suggest appropriate questions or strategies that may help them make better sense of the problem and/or how to represent the data given.

Examine the following student work. Think about the feedback you might give each student. Recall that effective feedback begins with a positive statement followed by nonjudgmental comments designed to move students along their learning progressions. Phrasing your feedback so that a one-word response is inappropriate will be helpful.

Student A

1. Ray had a block of wood in the shape of a rectangular prism. The block and its dimensions are shown below.

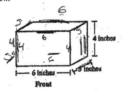

a. Ray painted the front face of the block red. What is the area of the face he painted red? Show or explain how you got your answer.

I think the area would be 20 because I added two side that are the same that was 6 inches and then I added the the other two sides that was 4 inches. = 6+6+4+4=20

Student A—*Continued*

b. Ray painted the top and bottom faces of the block black. What is the area

of the faces he painted black? Show or explain how you got your

answer. I think that the area would be
44 because What I did
was 3+5+5+5 = +5+5+5+5=
6+6+5+5=22
5+5+6+6 =+22
44

c. Ray painted the other faces of the block white. What is the area

of the faces he painted white? Show or explain how you got your answer.

I think the area would be 36 because what I
did was 4+4+5+5=18
5+5+4+4=18
36

Sample feedback might include the following:

- The labels for each dimension are accurate.

- Help me understand why you added the dimensions to find the area.

- I see that you added the dimension in part c, but I don't see any labels on the numbers. Help me understand what the values represent and how you know they are giving you an area.

- Can you explain to me the difference between area and perimeter?

Student B

1. Ray had a block of wood in the shape of a rectangular prism. The block and its
   dimensions are shown below.

a. Ray painted the front face of the block red. What is the area of
   the face he painted red? Show or explain how you got your answer.
   He painted 6 inches for red
   for the front.

b. Ray painted the top and bottom faces of the block black. What is the area
   of the faces he painted black? Show or explain how you got your
   answer. 5 inches for the top and
   bottom face. Black

c. Ray painted the other faces of the block white. What is the area
   of the faces he painted white? Show or explain how you got your answer.
   4 inches he painted of white.

Sample feedback might include the following:

- Would you please show me on a ruler how long 6 inches is?

- Does it make sense that Ray would paint only one 6-inch line on the prism?

- What do you think you need to do to find how much space he actually painted?

- What other strategies might you use to find the area?

- Explain to me how many dimensions the area has and what those dimensions are.

- Could you show what the face of the block is?

- What do you think this "6" refers to on the block? (Use the dimensions to help the child understand that the measurements refer to the length of the dimensions.)

Student C

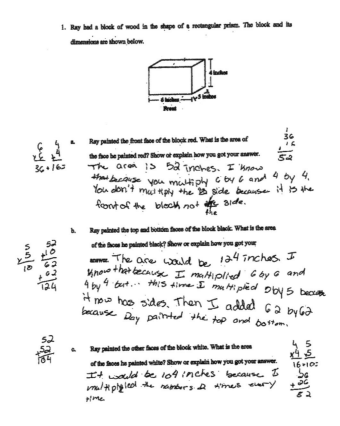

Sample feedback might include the following:

- I noticed that all your computations are correct.

- What was your strategy for solving this problem?

- Tell me what the difference is between inches and square inches.

- It would help me understand your computations if you drew a two-dimensional net and labeled all the sides appropriately.

Student D

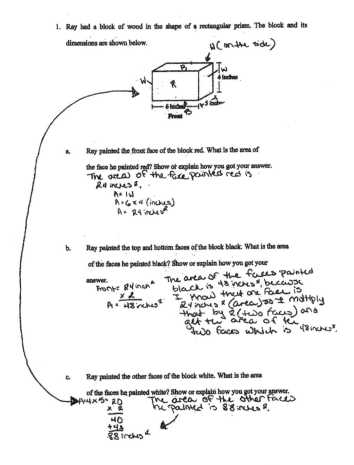

Sample feedback might include the following:

- The labels you used make it easy to understand your thinking.

- Help me understand how you found the dimensions of the top and bottom faces.

- I noticed that you found the area of the front face is 24 square inches. What is the area of the top face?

- What faces do you need to identify to find the sum of the areas that are painted white?

Linking assessment to instruction

You can use exit cards, gallery walks, interviews, or interventions based on student misconceptions to link assessment to instruction. To challenge students who need an extension, pose the following problems:

a. A cube falls into a bucket of paint and comes out covered on all 6 faces. The cube is then cut into smaller cubes, each 1 inch on an edge. If the original cube was 2 inches on each edge, how many pieces will there be? How many of those pieces will have paint on 3 faces? On 2 faces? On 1 face? On no faces?

b. Mrs. Collins had some white paint and some green paint and a bunch of wooden cubes. She asked some students to paint the cubes by making each face either solid white or green. Emma painted all her cube faces white. Abby painted all her cube faces green. Tim painted 4 faces white and 2 faces green. How many cubes could be painted so that each cube is totally different from the others?

Sample Exit Cards

- How might you determine the surface area of a cube that is 4 feet in length?
- How might you find the surface area of a rectangular prism with dimensions of 3 feet by 4 feet by 5 feet?
- Compare the surface area of a cube that is 6 feet long with the surface area of a rectangular prism with dimensions of 5 feet by 6 feet by 7 feet. Which object has the greater surface area?
- Draw a two-dimensional net for the rectangular prism with dimensions of 2 feet by 4 feet by 6 feet.

Problem 4: Graphing Data in a Circle

We are emphasizing students' prior knowledge through suggested range questions and sharing an effective instruction intervention should students misunderstand the range question.

A group of students were asked to choose their favorite sport. The results are given below. Display their choices in a circle graph. Show all steps.

Favorite sport	# of people
Hockey	18
Baseball	15
Basketball	9
Soccer	6

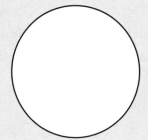

Curricular focus

This problem aligns with the following Focal Points, Principles and Standards, and Common Core State Standards.

Focal Point

Data analysis: Students apply percentages to make and interpret histograms and circle graphs.

Principles and Standards

Select, create, and use appropriate graphical representations of data.

Common Core State Standards

Construct viable arguments and critique the reasoning of others. Solve real-life and mathematical problems involving angle measure, area, surface area, and volume.

Assessing prior knowledge

Sample range questions:

a. Turn to your partner, and discuss and record what you both think a circle is.

b. Turn to your partner, and discuss and record how you might determine what portion of a circle graph a given value might have.

c. Turn to your partner, and discuss and record how you might find a percent value represented in a circle graph if you are given the number of degrees.

Assessing students at work

Ways to assess students include hinge questions, gallery walks, accountable talk, and observation protocols. Listening for accountable talk as students work is important.

- Ask the students to explain how they are determining the number of degrees for each sport.

- Ask the students to explain how they are determining the percentage for each sport and how that percentage relates to the size of the sector.

- Encourage students who demonstrate proficiency to pose other problems that can be solved using the same data.

- Set up a gallery walk and ask students to record their reasoning about circle graphs. Ideas you might include are central angle, how to find the percentage for a sector, and how to find the number of degrees in a sector.

Linking assessment to instruction

You can use exit cards, gallery walks, interviews, or interventions based on student misconceptions to link assessment to instruction. If most of the class could not correctly define what a circle is, they might have said, "a circle is something round"; you should take time to engage students in modeling how a circle is formed (see the following).

Give each student a blank, square piece of paper or card stock measuring about 6 inches by 6 inches, along with a ruler. Instruct your students to mark the center of the square with a dot. Next, prompt your students to draw as many 4-inch line segments as possible through the center point so that there are 2 inches on both sides of the center point. Continue drawing line segments through the center point until there is no more room. After an allotted time, ask the students to describe what they observe about their line segments. Place each student's observation on the conjecture board. Engage the students in refining the conjectures until they have determined that a circle is composed of endpoints that are equidistant from the center point. You may instruct the students to connect all the endpoints or to cut out the shape formed by the endpoints of the line segments.

Problem 5: Proportional Reasoning

The focus discussion for this problem is on the evidence seen in the student work. Most of the student work demonstrates the challenges and misconceptions students have reasoning proportionally. Querying students about their thinking is most often helpful.

> In the space below, draw two line segments, one of them 6 cm long and the other 10 cm long. Below this pair, draw another two segments that are of different lengths but proportional to the lengths of the first two segments.

Curricular focus

This problem aligns with the following Focal Points, Principles and Standards, and Common Core State Standards.

Focal Points

Measurement and Geometry: Students connect their work on proportionality with their work on area and volume by investigating similar objects. Students apply their work on proportionality to measurement in different contexts.

> **Principles and Standards**
>
> Apply appropriate techniques, tools, and formulas to determine measurements.
>
> **Common Core State Standards**
>
> Analyze proportional relationships and use them to solve real-world and mathematical problems. Recognize and represent proportional relationships between quantities. Decide whether two quantities are in a proportional relationship.

Assessing prior knowledge

Sample range questions:

a. Tell me what you think the term *similar* means.

b. How might you determine whether two polygons are similar?

c. Which of the following figures do you think are similar? Explain why.

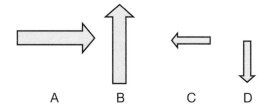

Assessing students at work

Ways to assess students include hinge questions, gallery walks, accountable talk, and observation protocols. Sample hinge questions may include the following:

a. You labeled some of these figures "congruent" and "similar." Can you tell me what you think it means for a figure to be congruent?

b. In what ways could you test congruency when the figures are not in the same orientation?

c. You said similar figures are "alike." Can you tell me more about what you are thinking?

d. I see that you are comparing the lengths of the figures. Can you help me understand how knowing the lengths will help you decide if the figures are congruent or similar?

e. Can you help me understand how or what you were thinking when you used the ratios you set up to decide which figures are similar?

Listen for accountable talk. Students should be encouraged to use appropriate mathematical language to include the terms *congruent* and *similar*.

Student thinking

For each of the following students we suggest appropriate questions or strategies that may help them make better sense of the problem and/or how to represent the data given.

Student A

In the space below, draw two line segments, one of them 6 cm long and the other 10 cm long. Below this pair, draw another two segments that are of different lengths, but proportional to the lengths of the first two segments.

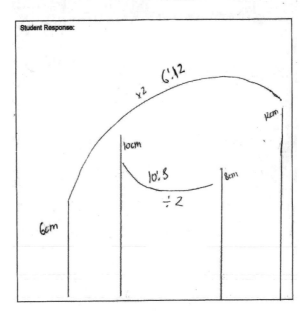

Student A has drawn parallel lines, the first of which is 6 cm and the second of which is 10 cm. The student is thinking multiplicatively as he multiplies the first length of 6 cm by a scale factor of 2 and draws a line segment that is 12 cm long. The student connects the 6-cm line segment to the 12-cm line segment and shows a ratio of 6:12. So far the student demonstrates understanding. However, as the student continues with the 10-cm line segment, he erroneously multiplies by a scale factor of $1/2$ (dividing by 2) and shows a ratio of 10:5. This action communicates a misconception.

This student would benefit from building lengths by using Cuisenaire rods, given various lengths coupled with various scale factors. The student may also benefit from drawing the line segments on graph paper to see how the same scale factor must be applied to each length.

Student B

In the space below, draw two line segments, one of them 6 cm long and the other 10 cm long. Below this pair, draw another two segments that are of different lengths, but proportional to the lengths of the first two segments.

Student Response:

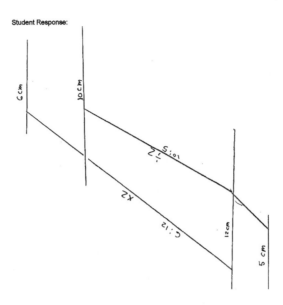

Student B demonstrates the same misconception as student A. As the illustration shows, this student applied a scale factor of 2 to the shorter dimension but a scale factor of $1/2$ to the longer length. In addition to the intervention mentioned for student A, both students may benefit from investigating what happens if they are given geometric shapes and asked to build similar shapes, given scale factors. For instance, use a rectangle as the original figure and apply a scale factor of 2. The student would apply the scale factor of 2 to both the length and width. For example:

This activity also illustrates that as the length and width are doubled, the area is enlarged by a scale factor of 4. Instruct the students to continue applying various scale factors and to record the scale factor, length, width, and area in a table to reinforce how the area increases by the square of the linear scale factor.

Student C

In the space below, draw two line segments, one of them 6 cm long and the other 10 cm long. Below this pair, draw another two segments that are of different lengths, but proportional to the lengths of the first two segments.

Student Response:

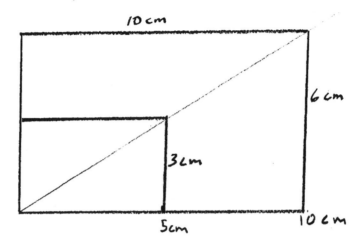

Student C used a geometric model to illustrate the given line segments. This student drew a diagonal from the far-left corner through the opposite vertex of the original dimensions, 6 cm by 10 cm, and then used the diagonal to draw a second rectangle with a scale factor of $^1/_2$. Instructing this student to share his thinking may also help the other students rethink their representations.

Student D

In the space below, draw two line segments, one of them 6 cm long and the other 10 cm long. Below this pair, draw another two segments that are of different lengths, but proportional to the lengths of the first two segments.

Student Response:

——————————————————— 10 cm

——————————— 6 cm

10 - 2 = 8 cm
6 - 2 = 4 cm

———————————— 8 cm

————— 4 cm

Student D made the most common error we saw across the student work. The student was not thinking multiplicatively but rather additively. The student subtracted 2 cm from each original line segment. This student misunderstands ratio and proportionality. The student may benefit from the interventions mentioned earlier as well as from doing more work with manipulatives to illustrate applying and checking the attributes of similarity.

Linking assessment to instruction

You can use exit cards, gallery walks, interviews, or interventions based on student misconceptions to link assessment to instruction.

Classroom activity: Give students various shapes, such as a rectangle, right triangle, parallelogram, and trapezoid. Instruct them to build shapes similar to the one shape they were given. They should build a shape that has a scale factor of 2, 3, and 4. Instruct the students to record their results in a table. Focus should be on comparing how the linear measures increase by a factor of 2, 3, and 4 while the area measures increase by a scale factor of 4, 9, and 16.

Problem 6: Proportional Reasoning

This problem examines student work with proportional reasoning through a gallery walk. Since students must transition from absolute or additive thinking to successfully reason through ratio and proportionality, they must have many experiences working with proportions. The student work highlights typical student misconceptions. Interactive lessons that engage students in making proportions a reality may overcome these misconceptions.

> Rick's box of cereal contains blue and purple marshmallows. He pours some cereal and sees 10 blue and 8 purple marshmallows in his bowl. The next morning, he pours himself a much larger bowl of cereal. If the new bowl has 108 marshmallows that are in the same ratio of blue to purple, how many blue and how many purple marshmallows are in the larger bowl?
>
> *Source:* Rock, David, and Mary Porter. "Palette of Problems." *Mathematics Teaching in the Middle School* 15 (October 2009): 132.

Curricular focus

This problem aligns with the following Focal Points, Principles and Standards, and Common Core State Standards.

Focal Points

Number and Operations and Algebra and Geometry: Developing an idea of and applying proportionality, including similarity. Students extend their work with ratios to develop an understanding of proportionality that they apply to solve single- and multistep problems in many contexts.

Principles and Standards

Develop, analyze, and explain methods for solving problems involving proportions, such as scaling and finding equivalent ratios.

Common Core State Standards

Analyze proportional relationships and use them to solve real-world and mathematical problems. Decide whether two quantities are in a proportional relationship. Recognize and represent proportional relationships between quantities.

Many students display misconceptions about proportions and proportional reasoning. If students have not transitioned from thinking additively to thinking multiplicatively, they will benefit from modeling problems, making rate tables, and graphing relationships to recognize that proportions involve a scale factor. The more experiences they have, the more likely they are to transition to thinking multiplicatively.

Student thinking

For each of the following students we suggest appropriate questions or strategies that may help them make better sense of the problem and/or how to represent the data given.

Student A

Student Response:

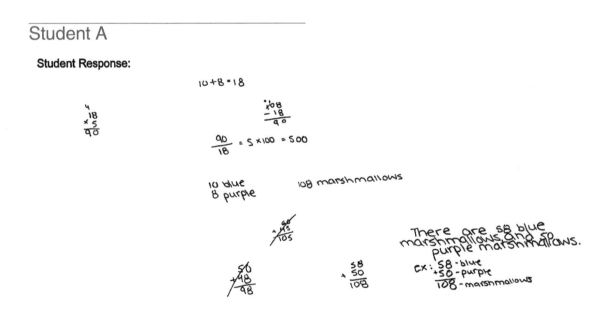

Most of the various computations displayed are addition. Student A appears to be guessing and checking values that will add to 108. The student labeled few numerical values. This student might be helped if asked to identify a strategy that could be used to solve the problem. Asking this student hinge questions such as the following while he worked definitely would have helped him: *Can you predict how many purple marshmallows there would be if you had 20 blue marshmallows? If you had 40 blue marshmallows, how many purple marshmallows would there be? If there were 72 purple marshmallows, how many blue marshmallows would there be?* Suggesting that the student organize his guesses into a table may have a positive impact on helping the student recognize that he should be thinking multiplicatively.

Student B

Student Response:

Blue to Purple

10:8 = 18 marshmallows.

60:48 = 108 marshmallows.

108 ÷ 18 = 6

10 × 6 = 60
8 × 6 = 48

Answer = 60:48

Student B demonstrates an understanding of the multiplicative relationship between the blue and purple marshmallows. However, instructing the students to justify or explain their reasoning would have been helpful. An extension might be to ask students to graph the relationship between the original ratio and the new ratio.

Student C

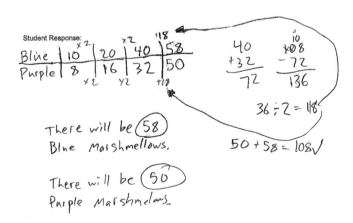

Student C began with a table, deciding that a scale factor of 2 was necessary. The student used the scale factor of 2 in the first three columns but then stopped multiplying. The student summed the rows, subtracted the sum from the goal of 108 marshmallows, and divided that difference by 2 to equally share the 36 marshmallows. The student went from thinking exponentially to thinking additively. This student is not alone in making this error: many students think that adding the same number to a ratio maintains the ratio. Perhaps this misconception originates in students' not understanding that multiplying by 2 is not the same as adding 2. This fact is not obvious if the children use the number 2 as a starting value since 2×2 and $2 + 2$ yield the same result. This situation warrants an interview with the student to determine his reasoning and sense making.

Teacher: I really am impressed that you organized your thinking by using a table. I noticed you began your table by multiplying the original 10 blue marshmallows and the 8 purple marshmallows by 2. Would you explain what you were thinking when you did this?

Student: I know I need a total of 108 marshmallows, and I know that the starting ratio of 10 blue to 8 purple means a fraction of 10/8, and I can multiply the numerator and denominator by 2 to get an equivalent ratio.

Teacher: I see, but if you multiplied the equivalent ratio by 2, by what is the original ratio being multiplied?

Student: I didn't multiply the original ratio again. I don't know what you mean.

Teacher: If you compare the ratio of 10/8 to 40/32, what scale factor did you use?

Student: The scale factor was 2 . . . oh, I see, I multiplied by 2×2 and then I added. I don't think I did it right.

Teacher: Go back and try solving it again. Think about how you can use your table differently to help you find the correct ratio.

Student D

Student Response:

108 ÷ 2 = 54

54 : 54

54 blue : 54 purple

The new bowl has 54 blue marshmallows and 54 purple marshmallows.

Student D demonstrates a misconception about the relationship between the blue and purple marshmallows. Does this student understand what a ratio represents? The student would benefit from hinge questions designed to encourage the student to model the original problem, such as the following: *What does a ratio of 10 blue to 8 purple look like? If a scale factor of three was applied to this ratio, what happens? What do you think you would have to do to the blue tiles if the purple tiles grew to be four times as large?* Colored tiles (use red instead of purple) or small pieces of colored paper would be suitable manipulatives to help the child understand that he can find the original ratio of 10 to 8 in any of the models built. For example, build a model to show a ratio of 8 blue to 10 purple tiles. Next ask the child to build a model of 30 blue tiles and 24 red tiles and ask the student to show you how they relate to the ratio of 8 to 10. These quantities should be deconstructed into three groups showing that the 10-to-8 relationship is constant and that this is what is producing the final quantity of each color. The student should also be encouraged to organize the data generated by the tiles or paper in a table or chart. The student should be prompted to identify patterns that developed and how those patterns can help answer the question posed in this problem.

Linking assessment to instruction

You can use exit cards, gallery walks, interviews, or interventions based on student misconceptions to link assessment to instruction.

When students struggle to develop understanding of an abstract concept, it usually means they have passed through the concrete and pictorial stages too quickly. Collins and Dacey (2010b) suggest using a Cuisenaire rod and an overhead projector to engage students in experimenting with ratios and proportions. Students place a red Cuisenaire rod on the plate of the overhead projector and project it onto a white screen or surface. They are challenged to determine the ratio of the projected image. Students then experiment with how they can project an image that is twice as large as the original, three times as large, and so on, and to record the various dimensions in a table. Students are asked to explain the patterns they developed through the experiment.

Sample Exit Cards

- List three things you know about proportions.
- Explain what a scale factor is.
- Explain what it means when a fraction is representing a ratio.

REFERENCES

Collins, Anne, and Linda Dacey. "Fact Practice." *Zeroing In on Number and Operation: Key Ideas and Misconceptions. Grades 7–8.* Portland, Maine: Stenhouse Publishers, 2010a.

———. "Reasoning Proportionally." *Zeroing In on Number and Operation: Key Ideas and Misconceptions. Grades 7–8.* Portland, Maine: Stenhouse Publishers, 2010b.

Chapter 5

Grade 8 Sample Problems Aligned with Curriculum Focal Points

IN ALIGNMENT with the Common Core State Standards mathematical practices, we encourage you to engage your students in making sense of problems and persevering in solving them, reasoning abstractly and quantitatively, constructing viable arguments, modeling with mathematics, using appropriate tools strategically, and attending to precision.

This chapter offers samples of effective classroom practices driven by the challenges and misconceptions articulated in sample student work. The approaches we include are gallery walks, preassessment strategies, strategies for assessing students at work, exit card sample questions, and teaching strategies designed to clarify student thinking and develop understanding.

Problem 1: Algebraic Thinking

The main focus in most grade 8 classrooms is on algebra or algebraic concepts. Definitions of what algebra is varies among mathematicians and mathematics educators, but Driscoll (1999, p. 1) describes algebra as "a type of reasoning in which one investigates the relationships between specific cases and possible generalizations and develops algebraic 'habits of mind'—ways of thinking about algebraic questions." The focus for this problem is student thinking and the strategies they use to solve the problem.

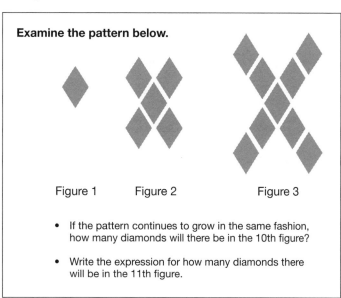

Examine the pattern below.

Figure 1   Figure 2   Figure 3

- If the pattern continues to grow in the same fashion, how many diamonds will there be in the 10th figure?

- Write the expression for how many diamonds there will be in the 11th figure.

Curricular focus

This problem aligns with the following Focal Points, Principles and Standards, and Common Core State Standards.

Focal Points

Algebra: Analyzing and representing linear functions and solving linear equations and systems of linear equations. Students use linear functions, linear equations, and systems of linear equations to represent, analyze, and solve a variety of problems. They view arithmetic sequences, including those arising from patterns or problems, as linear functions whose inputs are counting numbers.

Principles and Standards

Represent and analyze mathematical situations and structures by using algebraic symbols. Use symbolic algebra to represent situations and to solve problems, especially those that involve linear relationships.

Common Core State Standards

Understand the connections between proportional relationships, lines, and linear equations. Analyze and solve linear equations.

Assessing prior knowledge

Sample range questions:

a. How might you determine whether the following table is linear or nonlinear?

Input	1	2	3	4	5
Output	0	1	3	7	15

b. How might you describe a linear relationship?

c. Given the following table, determine whether it is linear or quadratic and explain how you know.

Input	1	2	3	4	5
Output	1	4	9	16	15

d. Write the following expression by using mathematical notation (do not read this aloud to your students): "Three more than five times eight."

Assessing students at work

Ways to assess students include hinge questions, gallery walks, accountable talk, and observation protocols.

Listen for accountable talk. Encourage students to include appropriate mathematical language that uses the terms *pattern, multiplicative, input–output, linear, finite difference,* and *order of operations.*

Student thinking

For each of the following students we suggest appropriate questions or strategies that may help them make better sense of the problem and/or how to represent the data given.

Student A

Examine the pattern below.

| Figure 1 | Figure 2 | Figure 3 |

- If the pattern continues to grow in the same fashion, how many diamonds will there be in the 10th figure?
- Write an expression for how many diamonds there will be in the nth figure.

A. In the 10th figure there will be 37 diamonds.

B. ~~~~~~~~

$$d = f - 1 \times 4 + 1$$

(d = diamonds f = figure number)

Student A wrote the correct answer but could not write a mathematical expression or equation to represent the generalized form for this pattern. Asking this student hinge questions to help him reason through writing an expression would be helpful. Sample hinge questions may include the following:

a. Help me understand what you were thinking when you wrote the equation $d = f - 1 \times 4 + 1$.

b. What solution do you think you would get if you substituted a 1 into your formula? Test your prediction.

c.   Would you agree that if you had no figures, you would have 0 diamonds? Test, for me, your formula for 0 figures. Do you get 0 diamonds?

d.   Help me understand how you might revise your formula so that it better represents what is happening as the pattern grows.

Student B

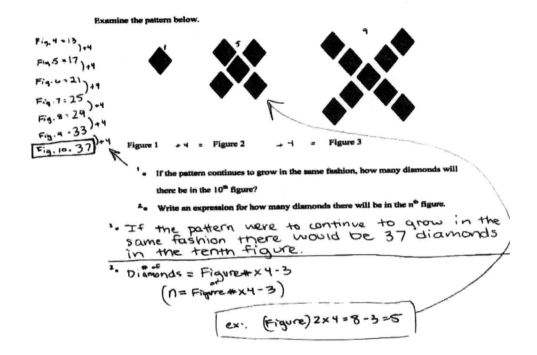

Student B has correctly identified the pattern but may benefit from conversation about the conventional manner in which an expression is written. The student defines n as "figure 2 × 4." The student may benefit from a conversation about mathematical conventions that would use the term n in the equation. More important is one of the most common misconceptions students make: stringing equations. Observe how the student lists "(Figure) 2 × 4 − 3 = 8 − 3 = 5."

This student would also benefit from being asked hinge questions while working through the problem. Sample hinge questions may include the following:

a.   I am curious about your equation. Please explain to me how you decided to use this notation.

b.   Help me understand why, after you defined n as "(Figure) 2 × 4 − 3," you didn't use the n in the equation.

c.   Let's examine your equation together. If I put my thumb over the 8 − 3, does the remaining equation, "(Figure) 2 × 4 − 3 = 5," make sense? What might you do to make this a true statement?

Student C

Examine the pattern below.

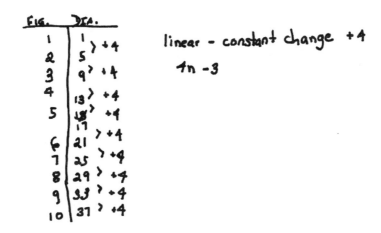

Figure 1   Figure 2   Figure 3

- If the pattern continues to grow in the same fashion, how many diamonds will there be in the 10th figure?

- Write an expression for how many diamonds there will be in the nth figure.

FIG.	DIA.	
1	1	+4
2	5	+4
3	9	+4
4	13	+4
5	17	+4
6	21	+4
7	25	+4
8	29	+4
9	33	+4
10	37	+4

linear - constant change +4

$4n - 3$

Student C answered the question correctly, showed how she used finite differences to determine that the expression was linear, and accurately wrote the expression. This student might do well by being challenged to pose her own pattern problems.

Linking assessment to instruction

You can use exit cards, gallery walks, interviews, or interventions based on student misconceptions to link assessment to instruction.

Classroom intervention: Many students may benefit from using a graphic organizer (see the following) that provides a nudge for how to best represent the problem. Students are instructed to use the graphic organizer to illustrate their thinking by using a table, graph, equation, or window settings on a graphing calculator and explaining or justifying their work. Once students internalize the ritual of thinking about multiple representations, encourage them to use the most appropriate representation for each problem.

Table	Graph
Equation Window Settings on a Graphing Calculator	Justify your answer

Including a graphic organizer similar to the one shown here offers yet another venue for formative assessment. The type of graph the student makes will tell you about a student's proficiency in adapting the correct type of a graph for a given contextual situation. Including the window settings on a graphing calculator challenges students to determine which quadrant(s) is necessary to best represent the data in a given contextual situation. What the students represent in the chart can guide teacher–student conversations.

Sample Exit Cards

- How might you determine whether a pattern is linear or nonlinear?
- Make two input–output machines, one that is linear and one that is nonlinear. Explain how you know the difference.
- Pose a pattern problem for a classmate to solve.

Problem 2: Interpreting Data and Identifying Linear Equations

This algebra problem assesses students' abilities to interpret data from a table and use that information to identify the equation of a line, the slope, and the *y*-intercept. Students in grade 8 are expected to model the relationships between and among data, testing to determine whether the relationship is linear or nonlinear. They should be engaged in describing situations that are linear or nonlinear and use finite differences to determine whether data in a table are linear.

The data in the table show the cost of renting a bicycle by the hour, including a deposit.

Renting a Bicycle

Hours (h)	Cost in dollars (c)
2	15
5	30
8	45

If hours, h, were graphed on the horizontal axis and cost, c, were graphed on the vertical axis:
- Are the data linear or nonlinear? How do you know?
- What is the equation of the line that best fits the data?
- If the data are linear, what is the slope of this line?
- What is the y-intercept?

Source: Adapted from STAR (Standardized Testing and Reporting), California Department of Education, Sample Test Questions, Grade 8, 2009

Curricular focus

This problem aligns with the following Focal Points, Principles and Standards, and Common Core State Standards.

Focal Points

Algebra: Analyzing and representing linear functions and solving linear equations and systems of linear equations. Students use linear functions, linear equations, and systems of linear equations to represent, analyze, and solve a variety of problems.

Principles and Standards

Represent and analyze mathematical situations and structures by using algebraic symbols. Use symbolic algebra to represent situations and to solve problems, especially those that involve linear relationships.

Common Core State Standards

Understand the connections between proportional relationships, lines, and linear equations. Analyze and solve linear equations.

Assessing prior knowledge

Sample range questions:

a. Given data in a table, how might you determine whether the relationship is linear?

b. Given data in a table that are linear, how might you determine the slope?

c. The total cost, c, in dollars of renting a motor scooter for d days is given by the equation $c = 130 + 25d$. List everything you can determine from the equation.

d. List everything you can for the expression $a^2 - 25$.

Assessing students at work

Ways to assess students include hinge questions, gallery walks, accountable talk, and observation protocols.

Listen for accountable talk. Encourage students to include appropriate mathematical language that uses the terms *slope*, *y-intercept*, *linear*, *variable*, *table*, *independent variable*, and *dependent variable*.

Gallery walk: Hang a series of easel-sized paper sheets with various tables around the room. (See the following sample tables.) For each table, instruct the students to do the following:

- Identify whether the data represented are linear or nonlinear.

- Write an equation of the line represented by the data if possible.

- Sketch a graph that best represents the data in the table.

- Create two questions that someone might ask about each table or create a situation that any table representing a linear relationship can describe.

Sample tables follow (be sure to use variables other than x and y so that students realize that other variables act in the same manner as x and y and may better define the situation being represented):

s	t
−5	−23
0	−3
3	9
4	13
n	

c	d
6	−16
7	−19
9	−25
13	−37
n	

a	b
1	2
3	10
4	17
9	82
n	

m	n
1	1
2	3
3	7
4	15
n	

Use your observation protocol to determine which students show confidence with the mathematics and which students need further experiences with the different representations. For students who demonstrate proficiency, challenge them to write problems that the data in the tables could represent.

Student thinking

For each of the following students we suggest appropriate questions or strategies that may help
them make better sense of the problem and/or how to represent the data given.

Student A

The data in the table show the cost of renting a bicycle by the hour, including a deposit.

Renting a Bicycle

Hours (h)	Cost in dollars (c)
2	15
5	30
8	45

15

15

If hours, *h*, were graphed on the horizontal axis and cost, *c*, were graphed on the vertical

axis

- Is the data linear or non linear? How do you know?   +15

- What is the equation of line that best fits the data?   C = 15c

- If linear, what is the slope of this line?   m = 15

- What is the y-intercept?   (0,0)

Student A made one of the most common errors. Given a table, many students simply examine
its output section to determine what the relationship is, perhaps because most of their experiences
include an increase of 1 in the input. When the input increases by 1, students do not need to think
of the ratio between the input and the output; rather, they think additively instead of multiplicatively. Directions requesting that students explain their thinking or justify their work would also
have been helpful.

Student B

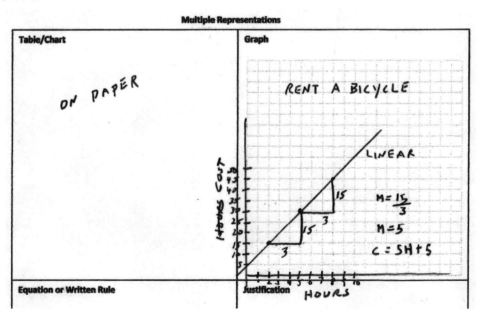

Student B chose to use a graph to determine whether the relationship is linear or nonlinear. The student appears to have drawn all her conclusions from the shape of the graph. The student also drew in the rise and the run, showed the ratio between them, and simplified the ratio and used that as the basis for the equation. It appears as if the student found the y-intercept by inspection. Again, since the problem did not require justification, we can only speculate on what the student was thinking.

Linking assessment to instruction

You can use exit cards, gallery walks, interviews, or interventions based on student misconceptions to link assessment to instruction.

Sample Exit Cards

- Explain at least two ways in which you can determine the slope of a line given a table with a constant rate of change.
- Explain what it means if you get a constant rate of change after finding a second finite difference in a data table.
- What are two different ways of thinking about the slope of a line?
- Does this table represent a linear or nonlinear relationship? Explain your reasoning.

r	s
0	5
4	8
7	11
10	14
14	17

- What are some considerations you must make when determining the equation of a line from a table? (Assume that the relationship is linear.)

Problem 3: Computing with Averages

Most students are assigned average problems that require them only to add and divide. This problem challenges students to think beyond the procedure and examine the information given. Few grade 8 students answered this correctly, and many demonstrated frustration with being asked to solve a problem they had not seen before. Many students simply wrote on their papers that the problem was too difficult for grade 8. Yet, as you will see in the sample of student work, students who understand averages solved the problem.

Donovan earned 89%, 87%, 91%, and 84% on tests 1, 2, 3, and 4, respectively, in his science class. If each test is worth 100 points and the final exam is worth 150 points, what percentage will Donovan need to earn on the final exam so that his overall average is 90%?

Curricular focus

This problem aligns with the following Focal Points, Principles and Standards, and Common Core State Standards.

Focal Points

Data Analysis and Number and Operations and Algebra: Analyzing and summarizing data sets. Students use descriptive statistics, including mean, median, and range, to summarize and compare data sets, and they organize and display data to pose and answer questions.

Principles and Standards

Select and use appropriate statistical methods to analyze data. Find, use, and interpret measures of center and spread, including mean and interquartile range.

Common Core State Standards

Recognize that a measure of center for a numerical data set summarizes all its values with a single number, whereas a measure of variation describes how its values vary with a single number.

Assessing prior knowledge

Sample range questions:

a. If you earned the following grades, would you prefer to have your teacher use the mean, median, or mode for your report card grade? Explain your thinking.

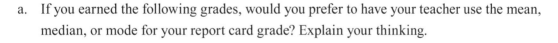

      75   91   85   39   75   83   100

b. Make a list of three different situations in which you think using the mean, median, or mode is more appropriate. Justify your response.

c. If you added a 100 to the following list of scores, which measure(s) of central tendency would most be affected—the mean, median, or mode? Explain your thinking.

      75   91   85   39   75   83   100

d. Which measure of central tendency balances all the data among the number of cases being examined? Explain what you think the balancing means.

Student thinking

For each of the following students we suggest appropriate questions or strategies that may help them make better sense of the problem and/or how to represent the data given.

Student A

3. Donovan earned 89%, 87%, 91%, and 84% on tests 1, 2, 3, and 4, respectively, in his science class. If each test is worth 100 points and the final exam is worth 150 points, what percentage will Donovan need to earn on the final exam so that his overall average is 90%?

$$89 + 87 + 91 + 84 = 351 \div 5 = 70.2$$

$$89 + 87 + 91 + 84 + 99 = 450 \div 5 \; \boxed{90}$$

To earn a 90% on his overall average he needs a 99 on the final exam

Student A demonstrates an understanding that finding averages (the mean) involves addition and division but does not appear to understand the concept underlying the formula. The student divided by 5 after adding four test scores and neglected to calculate what he needed for total points (400 + 150 = 550 points). The student then added 99, for a total of 450, which he then divided by 5 to get 90%. He neglected to calculate how many points he needed to get 90% of the total 550 points.

Sample feedback includes the following:

- Help me understand what averaging grades means.

- Explain to me what you were thinking when you added the score of 99 to the list. I am not sure where that score came from.

- If Donovan earned a 100% score on each assessment, what is the total number of points he would have earned? How might this information help you answer the question posed?

- Describe to me what happens when you are finding an average or mean. I don't want to know that you add and divide but rather what actually occurs during the process.

Student B

3. Donovan earned 89%, 87%, 91%, and 84% on tests 1, 2, 3, and 4, respectively, in his science class. If each test is worth 100 points and the final exam is worth 150 points, what percentage will Donovan need to earn on the final exam so that his overall average is 90%?

This problem is hard for me because I don't know how to work the "150 point test" part into want I want to do. If I were to answer this, I would answer, 99% on the 150 point test.

Student B simply expresses her inability to apply previous learning to this specific problem situation. The difficulty may be a language issue, or it might be a familiarity with the way other average problems have been posed. The student may benefit from a conversation about problem-solving strategies to include the following: solve a simpler problem, draw a picture, make a table, make an organized list, look for patterns, model the problem, make a graph, work backward, and guess and check. After identifying an appropriate strategy, the student would most likely benefit from solving the problem with a peer.

Sample feedback includes the following:

- Describe to me what an average represents.

- Tell me how many points one can earn in these five assessments.

- If one can earn 550 points, how might you determine how many points are necessary to average 90%? Do you know, or can you determine, what 90% of 550 is?

Student C

Donovan earned 89%, 87%, 91%, and 84% on tests 1, 2, 3, and 4, respectively, in her science class. If each test is worth 100 points and the final exam is worth 150 points, what percentage will Donovan need to earn on the final exam so that her overall average is 90%?

THERE ARE 550 POINTS ON ALL 6 TESTS $(100+100+100+100+150)$
SO FAR SHE GOT 351 POINTS $(89+87+91+84)$

IF HER AVERAGE FOR ALL 5 IS 90%
THEN SHE'LL HAVE 90% OF 550
OR 495 POINTS $(.90 \times 550)$

BUT SHE'S ALREADY GOT 351 So
SHE STILL NEEDS 144 MORE $(495-351)$

Student C—*Continued*

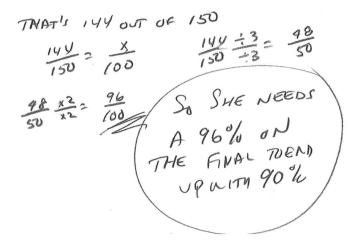

Student C correctly solved the problem and explained each step along the way. The student showed an understanding of averages (means) and proportions. The greatest difference between this student's work and most of the other work was his knowledge that a total of 550 points is possible across the five tests and that he needed to know what 90% of those 550 points is.

Sample feedback includes the following:

- Help me understand why you used a proportion.
- What does the average do to a set of data?
- If you had to describe how to find the average for a data set, what might you say? (Consider that this person knows the procedure of adding and dividing, but that is all.)

Linking assessment to instruction

You can use exit cards, gallery walks, interviews, or interventions based on student misconceptions to link assessment to instruction.

Classroom intervention: Since this problem proved difficult for so many students, using colored tiles to solve a simpler problem that includes the same level of challenge might help some students. You might challenge your students to model the following problem: *A carnival game challenged people to catch "fish" by using a magnetic fishing pole. After four separate trials, Aiden caught 8 fish, 7 fish, 9 fish, and 6 fish of a possible 10 fish each time. In the fifth trial, he moved to a new location and noticed 15 fish in the pond. How many fish will he need to catch to have an average of 80% fish caught?* Students will use the tiles to represent the total number of fish in the pond and the number they caught. They will also be expected to make sense of a rational-number answer.

Sample Exit Cards

- Explain in your own words the meaning of *average* or *mean*. (Do not tell me how to do it; rather, tell me what it really means.)
- If you earned the following scores on your math assessments this semester, would you like your teacher to tell your parents the mean, mode, or median score? Justify your response.

  91, 83, 72, 83, 87, 100, 45, 85
- Since the mathematical procedure for finding the mean is to add all data and divide by the number of data points, explain what really happens to the data when the average (mean) is found.

Problem 4: Inferring from Linear and Nonlinear Graphs

Interpreting graphs or writing stories about a graphical representation is an important component in algebraic reasoning. Too many students never get the opportunity to interpret graphs because the focus has been on generating the graphs given various data. By grade 8, students should be able to recognize linear and nonlinear graphs and distinguish linear graphs with a positive slope from those with a negative slope.

Identify a situation that each graph can represent. Label both axes to show the relationship.

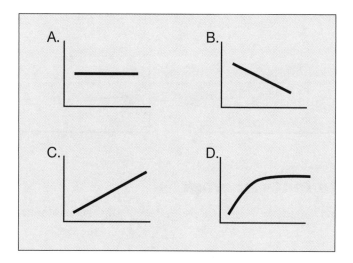

Curricular focus

This problem aligns with the following Focal Points, Principles and Standards, and Common Core State Standards.

Focal Points

Students encounter some nonlinear functions (such as the inverse proportions that they studied in grade 7 as well as basic quadratic and exponential functions) whose rates of change contrast with the constant rate of change of linear functions.

Principles and Standards

Identify functions as linear or nonlinear and contrast their properties from tables, graphs, or equations.

Common Core State Standards

Use functions to model relationships between quantities. Describe qualitatively the functional relationship between two quantities.

Assessing prior knowledge

Sample range questions:

   a. Describe the characteristics of a linear graph.

   b. Explain how to identify the independent axis and the dependent axis.

   c. Record everything you know about the following graphs.

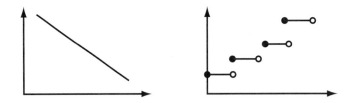

Assessing students at work

Ways to assess students include hinge questions, gallery walks, accountable talk, and observation protocols.

    Listen for accountable talk. Encourage students to include appropriate mathematical language that uses the terms *relationship*, *independent variable*, and *dependent variable*.

Student thinking

For each of the following students we suggest appropriate questions or strategies that may help them make better sense of the problem and/or how to represent the data given.

Student A

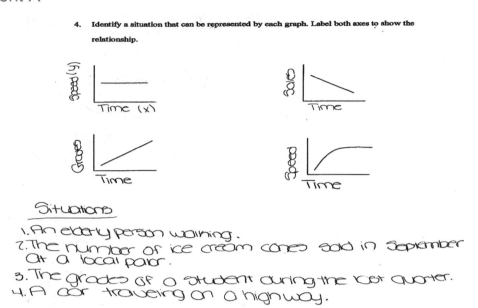

4. Identify a situation that can be represented by each graph. Label both axes to show the relationship.

Situations
1. An elderly person walking.
2. The number of ice cream cones sold in September at a local fair.
3. The grades of a student during the last quarter.
4. A car traveling on a highway.

Student A correctly labeled the axes for a relationship between speed and time. What "an elderly person walking" means in the description for the first graph is unclear. An interview with this student would be beneficial. The second graph erroneously indicates that the number of ice cream cones sold decreases over time rather than increases. The explanation for the third graph is not descriptive enough to convey what the student is thinking. The fourth graph also correctly labels the axes but does not explain what is happening with the car traveling on a highway. It is apparent that the student has not had a wealth of experiences describing situations on the basis of a graphical representation.

The responses to these graphs indicate a need to interview this student to fully understand what the child is thinking. Possible interview questions may include the following:

a. In graph A, could you explain what you mean by "an elderly person walking"?

b. How might a graph showing how a toddler walks look? Do you expect it to be different from that of an elderly person?

c. In graph B, you indicate that the number of cones sold decreases over time. Explain to me what you were thinking.

d. Is the number of cones decreasing over the course of a day realistic? Help me understand how that is possible.

e. In graph C, you give a vague description of what is happening with the grades. Why do you think the grades increase over time?

f. In graph D, you mention a car traveling on a highway. Describe to me how you see that car traveling.

g. Did you consider heavy volume of cars? Did you think about how the car traveling might be different if you are traveling late at night versus during rush hour or midafternoon? Please help me understand your thinking.

Student B

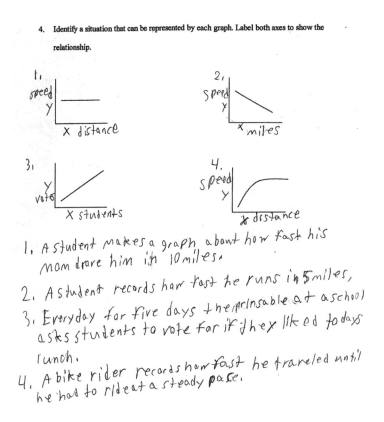

4. Identify a situation that can be represented by each graph. Label both axes to show the relationship.

1. A student makes a graph about how fast his mom drove him in 10 miles.

2. A student records how fast he runs in 5 miles.

3. Everyday for five days the principle at a school asks students to vote for if they liked to days lunch.

4. A bike rider records how fast he traveled until he had to ride at a steady pace.

Student B erroneously indicates that the speed at which his mother drives depends on the distance she travels. Whether the student is interpreting the horizontal line as the average rate of speed over the indicated distance or whether he thinks the speed at which she traveled was constant is unclear. The student neglects to indicate a rate of change in the speed from mile 0 to mile 10. In graph 2, the student again indicates that the speed depends on the distance. The work does not mention a constant decline—an important component in interpreting the graph. The student attributes graph 3, which shows a constant rate of change, to a survey of students. The described situation is not appropriate for this type of graph. Including a circle graph, a tally, or a bar graph would be more relevant. The student interprets the final graph as a rider bicycling at an increasing speed for a short distance, at which time the speed remained constant.

This student would benefit from various experiences, including generating data, representing that data with the most appropriate type of graph, and interpreting various types of graphs. You will also find out more about your students' thinking in an interview. Some suggested interview question are as follows:

a.　In graph 1, I'd like you to explain to me how the speed of the car depends on the distance that the car traveled.

b.　Will the distance that a car travels ever depend on the speed? Help me understand whether this is possible.

c. In graph 2, you also indicate that the speed depends on the distance. Do you think that the runner slows down at the same rate while running, or is it possible that the runner is inconsistent in his rate of speed? Help me understand.

d. In graph 3, you describe a situation that gives a frequency. What other types of graphs might you use to demonstrate a favorite food?

e. In graph 4, help me understand how the speed depends on the distance.

f. Is it possible that the distance that a person travels depends on the speed or the terrain? Explain your thinking.

Student C

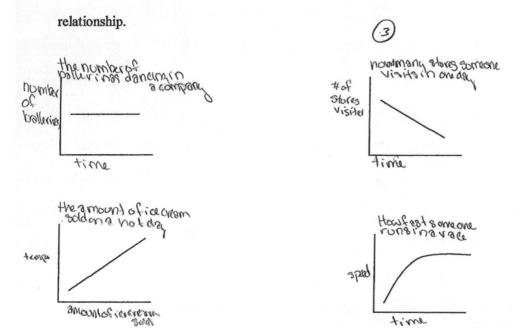

Student C appears to understand what is happening in all the graphs except for the graph labeled 3. Over time, the number of stores someone visits in one day should increase rather than decrease. This student may benefit from an immediate hinge question: *How can the number of stores you visited be fewer at the end of the day than the number you visited by noon?* The student appropriately labeled each axis, recognizing in three of the graphs that time is an independent variable. This student may benefit from working with more linear situations that have a negative slope to ensure full understanding.

Linking assessment to instruction

You can use exit cards, gallery walks, interviews, or interventions based on student misconceptions to link assessment to instruction.

Classroom intervention: Interpreting graphs causes difficulty for many students. The following activity helps students picture what a graph may represent. One teacher collects odd-shaped vases from yard sales and discount stores. None of the vases is extremely large, but all have interesting shapes. This teacher groups her class into threes to facilitate the activity. One student scoops colored water, a second student measures the amount of colored water in the vase, and the third student records the number of scoops and the measure of the water after each scoop. Students continue adding water, measuring the height of the water, and recording the number of scoops and the height of the water in the vase. When the vase is filled, the students work in their groups to first predict what they think a graph of the data will look like. After the prediction, the students graph the data from their scoops and water measure charts on easel paper. Students hang up their graphs in random order. The class then must decide which graph represents which vase.

Sample Exit Cards

- Sketch a graph that shows water draining from a bathtub. Be sure to label each axis.
- Sketch a graph that shows a family on a bicycle trip during which they begin at a steady rate, ride for a few hours, stop for a rest, begin riding up a steep hill, and continue riding over bumpy terrain until they stop for lunch. Be sure to label each axis.
- Sketch a graph of your choosing and write a story that explains the graph.

Problem 5: Graphing Data in a Circle

We highlighted this same problem for grade 7. After examining reams of student work, we concluded that many seventh-grade students did not have enough experience converting data from a table to a circle graph. We administered the same problem to students in grade 8 and still found serious misconceptions about how to mathematically translate data from a table to percents and those percents to degrees in a circle. Many students thought about the circle as a whole and divided it into fractional parts. Rarely did the student work indicate competency with identifying the number of degrees in the circle or the sectors. If the problem were scaffolded to ask students to specifically include the percent and the number of degrees included in each sector, the results might be different. However, scaffolding the question changes its cognitive demand. We are focusing on pre- and postassessments that may guide understanding of how to work with circle graphs.

A group of students were asked to choose their favorite sport. The results are given below. Display their choices in a circle graph. Show all steps.

Favorite Sport	No. of People
Hockey	18
Baseball	15
Basketball	9
Soccer	6

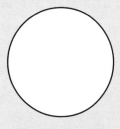

Source: Massachusetts Comprehensive Assessment

Curricular focus

This problem aligns with the following Focal Points, Principles and Standards, and Common Core State Standards.

Focal Points

Data Analysis: Students apply percentages to make and interpret histograms and circle graphs.

Principles and Standards

Select, create, and use appropriate graphical representations of data.

Common Core State Standards

Construct viable arguments and critique the reasoning of others. Solve real-life and mathematical problems involving angle measure, area, surface area, and volume.

Assessing prior knowledge

Sample range questions:

a. How many degrees are in a quarter of a circle?

b. If a pizza is divided into 4, 6, 8, 10, and 12 slices, with each slice of equal size, how many degrees are in the central angle of each slice? Justify your answers.

c. If 60° are in the central angle of a slice of pie and all the slices are the same size, what percent of the pie is represented? How do you know?

d. If 45° are in the central angle of a slice of pie and all the slices are the same size, what percent of the pie is represented? How do you know?

e. If 20° are in the central angle of a slice of pie and all the slices are the same size, what percent of the pie is represented? How do you know?

Assessing students at work

Ways to assess students include hinge questions, gallery walks, accountable talk, and observation protocols.

Listen for accountable talk. Encourage students to include appropriate mathematical language that uses the terms *central angle* and *degrees*.

Gallery walk: Post a variety of circles drawn on easel paper around the room. Each circle should be divided into different sectors. For instance, one circle would be divided into thirds, another into fifths, and a third into eighths. Instruct the students to post the number of degrees in each sector and tell what percent of the circle each sector represents.

Student thinking

Examine the following student work and think about the questions you might ask as they are working through the problem.

Student A

A group of students were asked to choose their favourite sport. The results are given below. Display their choices in a circle graph. Show all steps.

Favourite Sport	# People
Hockey	18
Baseball	15
Basketball	9
Soccer	6

37%.
31%.
17%.
12%.

first I added all of the sports' numbers together.
Then I took each of the numbers and divided it by
the sum which was 49. After I got an answer that was
a decimal I multiplied by 100 and rounded. Results:
• Hockey - 37%.
• baseball - 31%.
• basketball - 17%.
• soccer - 12%.

Student A—*Continued*

> Then I cut the circle in half which is 50%. I cut it in half again which is 25%. Hockey and baseball are around the same percent so they each got a 25% percent peice and a half of a 25% percent, one being a little bit larger than the other. Basketball and soccer were pretty close so soccer got a half of the 25% peice and basketball got a little bit more.

Student A began appropriately by finding the whole and identifying the percent that each part represented. The work shows some computational or rounding errors, but the underlying understanding of the concept thus far is clear. This student used his understanding about fractions to divide the circle and estimate the size of each sector. The work made no mention about converting the percent of the circle to its equivalent number of degrees in the circle.

Sample hinge questions may include the following:

a. Help me understand what the whole circle represents.

b. How should the percentages of each sport in the table be represented by the area in a circle?

c. I noticed you indicated that the percentage of people who preferred hockey was 37%, so can you explain to me why hockey received only 25% of the circle?

d. Can you explain to me how many degrees are in a circle?

Student B

A group of students were asked to choose their favourite sport. The results are given below. Display their choices in a circle graph. Show all steps.

Favourite Sport	# People
Hockey	18
Baseball	15
Basketball	9
Soccer	6

`50`

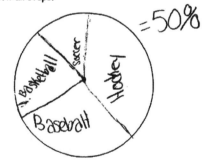

Student B—*Continued*

Turn to your partner, explain and then record below how you might determine what part of the circle graph a given sport will occupy.

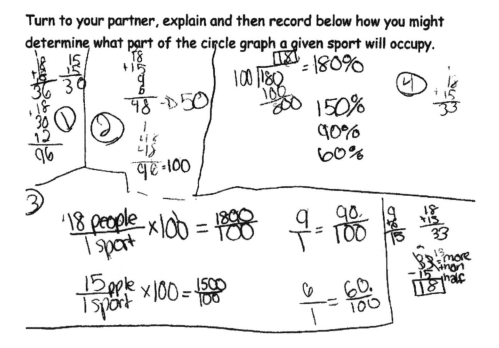

·I found out what amount of people surveyed   BART
·Then I found the percent
·I knew that all the people were about 50
·Then I added up hockey,18, & Baseball,15, which was 33. And then I added up Basketball,9, and Soccer,6, which was 15
·Then I subtracted 15 from 33 to find out if baseball and hockey was more than half together
·It was so then I had an Idea of where the lines would be

The graph that student B made is approximately correct. This student recognized that soccer plus hockey takes up half the circle and that baseball and basketball also require half the circle. This student added the number of people surveyed but, rather than working with that total, rounded up to 50 people. The student's computations are accurate until step 3. This student misunderstands how to multiply fractions by whole numbers, equivalences, and how the percent of a circle relates to the number of degrees in a circle.

Sample hinge questions may include the following:

a. Help me understand why you rounded the total number of people surveyed to 50.

b. I noticed that you put "= 50" next to the circle; tell me how that 50 relates to the table and the circle.

c. Can you tell me how the area of the circle relates to the data in the table?

d. How might you best use the circle to represent the data from the table in the circle?

e. You subtracted the number of people preferring basketball and soccer from hockey and baseball; help me understand how that helped you know where to draw the lines.

f. Your step 3 is interesting; please explain what you were thinking.

g. I noticed that you subtracted 15 from 33. What information did this give you? What were you thinking when you did this?

Student C

A group of students were asked to choose their favourite sport. The results are given below. Display their choices in a circle graph. Show all steps.

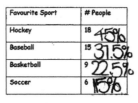

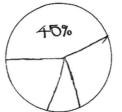

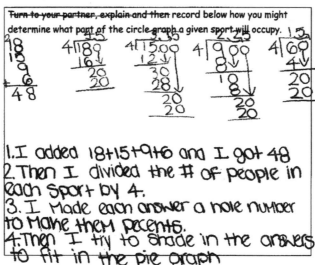

Student C misunderstands what finding the percent of a whole means. The student explains the computation but does not explain or justify those computations.

Sample hinge questions may include the following:

a. If there are a total of 48 people, what percentage of people does that represent?

b. Help me understand what the sum of 48 means for the circle. In other words, how might you decide how many degrees of the circle you need to represent the sum of 48 people?

c. Explain to me why you divided the number of people in each sport by 4. What information did the division give you?

Student D

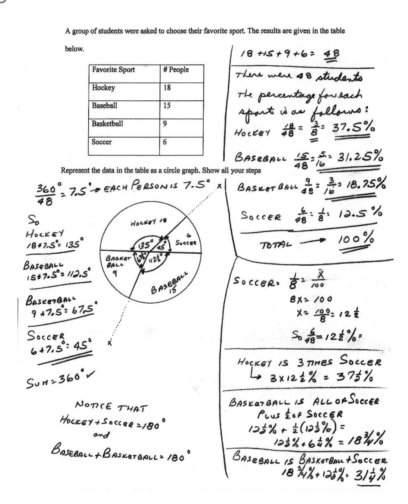

Student D correctly determined the percentage of students who preferred each sport and checked to ensure that the percents totaled 100%. This student also correctly converted each percent into the corresponding number of degrees in the circle that each preference would take. The student included a check to ensure that the total number of degrees is 360 and went one step forward to illustrate that two of the preferences added to 180 degrees. What is powerful about the work in the example is how the student used previous information, the value for soccer, to build later arguments. For example, the student found that soccer was $1/8$ of the total, with hockey being three times that amount. Basketball is all of soccer plus another half. Baseball is basketball plus soccer. The work in this response illustrates what having "number sense" at this grade level means.

Linking assessment to instruction

You can use exit cards, gallery walks, interviews, or interventions based on student misconceptions to link assessment to instruction.

Assign your students a project where they have to conduct a survey. You may want to do this activity in collaboration with the science teacher to ascertain that your students understand how to frame a research question that includes an "other" category. You may ask your students to interview more than 120 students to determine which of five recently released films is their favorite or what their favorite ice cream flavor or video game is. Once the students have determined the questions, instruct them to conduct the survey; record their results in a tally, in a circle graph, and in a bar graph; and create two questions that can be asked about the data. You may instruct them to complete the project on poster boards, which can be hung up around the classroom. Also instruct them to include all their calculations, both the degrees and percents for the circle graph, and whether the students think that labeling the circle graph in degrees or percents is more persuasive.

Title Name	H.R.
Tally	Bar Graph
Circle Graph	Conclusions

Problem 6: Solving Systems of Linear Equations

For grade 8, both *Curriculum Focal Points* and the Common Core State Standards emphasize including systems of linear equations that model actual contextual situations. For students in middle school, contextual systems are most appropriate. Often, the language in problems that include systems of equations confuses students, so it is important that accountable talk by teachers and students is included and expected. This problem focuses on multiple representations.

Ryan and Ashley are math tutors. Ryan charges $20 for the initial tutoring consultation to assess the learner and $8 per hour for tutoring. Ashley does not charge for the initial consultation but charges $10 per hour for tutoring. Mrs. Hernandez is looking for a math tutor for 4 weeks at 2 hours per week for her son. Which tutor will be less expensive? Who will be less expensive if she asks for tutoring for 4 hours per week for 4 weeks? At what point (in hours) will the cost of Ryan's services equal that of Ashley's?

Source: Rock, David, and Mary Porter. "Palette of Problems." *Mathematics Teaching in the Middle School* 15 (October 2009): 133.

Curricular focus

This problem aligns with the following Focal Points, Principles and Standards, and Common Core State Standards.

Focal Points

Algebra: Analyzing and representing linear functions and solving linear equations and systems of linear equations. Students use linear functions, linear equations, and systems of linear equations to represent, analyze, and solve a variety of problems.

Principles and Standards

Use symbolic algebra to represent situations and to solve problems, especially those that involve linear relationships

Common Core State Standards

Analyze and solve pairs of simultaneous linear equations. Solve real-world and mathematical problems leading to two linear equations in two variables.

Assessing prior knowledge

Sample range questions:

a. Write down what you think the term *breaking even* means.

b. What might the point (0, $32) mean when graphed on a Cartesian coordinate plane?

c. Suppose that two lines intersect at one point; what might that represent?

d. How many solutions exist to a system of equations if the lines are parallel to one another?

e. How many solutions exist to a system of equations if both equations are graphed but the graph has only one line?

f. Identify situations for each graph that best represent what is happening.

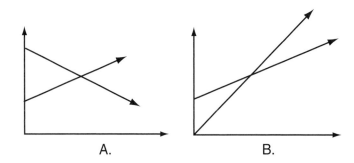

A.   B.

Assessing students at work

Ways to assess students include hinge questions, gallery walks, accountable talk, and observation protocols.

Listen for accountable talk. Encourage students to include appropriate mathematical language that uses the terms *slope of the line*, *positive slope*, *negative slope*, *steepness of the line*, *linear*, *y-intercept*, *intersection*, *constant rate of change*, *increasing*, and *decreasing*.

Observation protocol: Listen for which students use appropriate mathematical vocabulary. Watch for students who can work through the problem with little or no assistance and students who rely on others to make sense of the problem. Identify students who include multiple representations for the problem and those who do not use an appropriate graph for the problem.

Student thinking

For each of the following students we suggest appropriate questions or strategies that may help them make better sense of the problem and/or how to represent the data given.

Student A

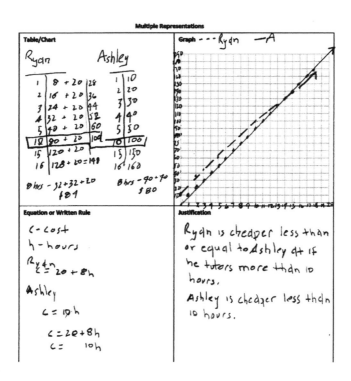

Student A used a graphic organizer that required students to use multiple representations. This student correctly made tables to show that the cost for tutoring 10 hours was the same for both Ryan and Ashley. Because of an error in listing the intervals on the *y*-axis, the breakeven point is misrepresented. The student neglected to title the graph and label the axes but did remember to include a legend for the lines. The student also correctly wrote the two equations. The student justification is weak. The work shows only the conclusion, not a mathematical argument.

Student B

Illustrate – Compute – Explain*
(I – C – E)
Illustrate(draw a picture, a diagram, a table, or a graph)

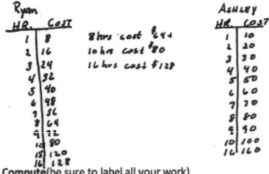

Ryan
HR.	COST
1	8
2	16
3	24
4	32
5	40
6	48
7	56
8	64
9	72
10	80
15	120
16	128

8 hrs cost $64
10 hrs cost $80
16 hrs cost $128

ASHLEY
HR.	COST
1	10
2	20
3	30
4	40
5	50
6	60
7	70
8	80
9	90
10	100
16	160

Compute(be sure to label all your work)

C = 8h   Ryan

C = 10h   ASHLEY

Explanation (explain the reasonableness of your answer or a justification for your solution)

Ryan is cheaper as a tutor. Ryan charges $64 for 8 hours and Ashley charges $80. For 16 hours Ryan charges $128 and Ashley charges $160

Student B made two tables that correctly indicate the cost per hour. The student neglected to include the one-time $20 fee that Ryan charged. On the basis of the omission of the $20, the cost for Ryan is less in both instances, but if the cost were added in, the total would be cheaper for Ashley up to ten hours. The omission is obvious in the equation representing Ryan's fees.

Student C

Ryan

HOURS	1	2	3	4	5	8	12	16
COST	20+8 28	20+16 36	20+24 44	20+32 52	20+40 60	20+64 84	20+80 100	20+128 148

Student C—*Continued*

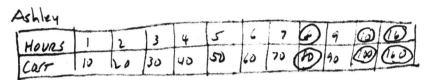

Ryan costs more if he tutors fewer than 10 hours. At
10 hours they both cost the same. Ashley costs more if
she tutors more than 10 hours.

Student C correctly represented the fees and total cost for both parties. The student also arrived at the correct conclusion that the number of hours is the determining factor for deciding which tutor is less expensive.

Linking assessment to instruction

You can use exit cards, gallery walks, interviews, or interventions based on student misconceptions to link assessment to instruction.

Sample Exit Cards

- What does the term *breaking even* mean?
- If two lines on a graph intersect, what does that mean?
- If two lines on a graph are parallel, what does that mean?
- How might you determine which value in a relationship is graphed on the *y*-axis?

Classroom intervention: If some students in your classes cannot relate to the fact that a *y*-intercept can be any point on the *y*-axis, not just at (0, 0), engaging them in a hands-on activity is beneficial to help them understand situations that have *y*-intercepts that are above (0, 0). Teachers have successfully used many experiments, including but not limited to measuring the extension of a helical spring (a "Slinky") with a cup attached. A constant weight is then added to the cup and the extension of the Slinky is measured again. This process continues for about six weights (when the physical properties of the Slinky change), and the data are recorded in a table or chart and graphed on the Cartesian coordinate plane. The experiment continues with students being instructed to crimp the Slinky in half and repeat the process with half the Slinky. The data are also graphed on the same set of axes. Students are asked to compare the two tables and graphs, to explain why the *y*-intercept is not at (0, 0), and to write an equation for a line if the data are linear (Collins and Dacey 2010).

References

Collins, Anne, and Linda Dacey. "Solving Problems with Proportionality." *Zeroing In on Number and Operation: Key Ideas and Misconceptions. Grades 7–8.* Portland, Maine: Stenhouse Publishers, 2010.

Driscoll, Mark. *Fostering Algebraic Thinking: A Guide for Teachers, Grades 6–10.* Portsmouth, N.H.: Heinemann, 1999.

Professional Development Guide

....

Ow do teachers become proficient with using formative assessment to move students' thinking and mathematical reasoning to greater levels of sophistication? "To achieve the best results with students when teaching for the depth, understanding, and proficiency sought by the curriculum focal points, teachers themselves will need a deep understanding of the mathematics and facility with the relationships among mathematical ideas. Thus, effective instruction built on the curriculum focal points requires in-depth preparation of preservice teachers and ongoing professional development for in-service teachers" (National Council of Teachers of Mathematics [NCTM] 2006, p. 7).

Why Do We Need More Professional Development?

Teachers' beliefs about mathematics are grounded in their own experiences as learners (Stigler and Hiebert 1998). Many teachers have never experienced mathematics as *mathematizing* (Fosnot and Dolk 2007). They have never explored and created mathematics or had the opportunity to communicate, defend, and revise their ideas as part of a community of discourse. Rather, their experience of learning mathematics was of a traditional instructional model: watch the teacher do a few computation or procedural problems and then do many similar problems silently at a desk. This model rewarded speed and memorization, and talking with classmates about math was the equivalent of cheating. The kind of thinking required to complete the tasks was at a low level of cognitive demand: memorization and procedures without connections (Smith and Stein 1998). Students could and usually did receive good grades for completing tasks quickly and accurately, with no need to demonstrate understanding of concepts underlying the procedures or to make mathematical connections or representations. People who are products of a traditional instructional style typically did not have the opportunity to explore mathematical ideas and were understandably left to assume that "getting the right answer" was the same as understanding math—or that they were faking their way through math class because they were good at memorizing. It's not surprising, then, that many current students' experiences in mathematics, despite standards-based curricula, parallel those of their teachers.

Mathematical Tasks with Higher Levels of Cognitive Demand

Procedures with connection tasks do the following:

- Focus students' attention on using procedures to develop deeper levels of understanding of mathematical concepts and ideas.

- Suggest pathways to follow (explicitly or implicitly) that are broad, general procedures that have close connections to underlying conceptual ideas, as opposed to narrow algorithms that are opaque with respect to underlying concepts.

- Usually are represented in multiple ways (e.g., visual diagrams, manipulatives, symbols, problem situations). Making connections among multiple representations helps to develop meaning.

- Require some degree of cognitive effort. Although general procedures may be followed, students cannot follow them mindlessly. To successfully complete the task and develop understanding, students need to engage with the conceptual ideas that underlie the procedures.

Carrying out mathematics tasks does the following:

- Requires complex and nonalgorithmic thinking (i.e., nothing in the task, task instructions, or a worked-out example explicitly suggests a predictable, well-rehearsed approach or pathway to use in solving the problem).

- Requires students to explore and understand the nature of mathematical concepts, processes, or relationships.

- Demands monitoring or regulating one's own cognitive processes.

- Requires students to access relevant knowledge and experiences and make appropriate use of them in working through the task.

- Requires students to analyze the task and actively examine task constraints that may limit possible solution strategies and solutions.

- Requires considerable cognitive effort and may involve some level of anxiety for the student owing to the unpredictable nature of the solution process required.

Teachers' own experiences as learners both directly and indirectly influence how they teach mathematics. Because teachers' own mathematics education may have typically been procedural, they tend to have a sketchy understanding of the big ideas in mathematics. If teachers do not know how mathematical ideas are connected and build on one another, how do teachers help children develop these during math learning? If teachers have a limited understanding of the big ideas in mathematics, how can they possibly recognize these ideas in students' talk and written work? And if teachers as learners are uncomfortable with being confused or being in a state of disequilibrium, how can they create learning environments where struggle is a natural and important part of the learning process?

This situation creates a deadening cycle: the superficial understanding of the process of doing mathematics results in less than creative ways of teaching mathematics, which results in a superficial understanding of mathematics. We can break this cycle only by changing how we teach. To do so, we must relearn mathematics in ways that develop a different understanding of what mathematics is and what it means to learn and teach mathematics. Teachers need to experience mathematics at high levels of cognitive demand: they must be immersed in problem solving, be challenged to refine and revise their ideas, and be expected to find ways to communicate and defend their ideas orally and in writing as part of a community of discourse.

Teachers also need to understand the process of developing mathematical thinking: what the big ideas are in mathematics and how students develop them. Traditional instructional methods do not invite students to explain their reasoning, reflect on connections between mathematical ideas, or reveal their thinking. To understand students' mathematical development, teachers must first give students opportunities to show their thinking. Teachers then need to hear the underlying mathematical ideas when students share their thinking orally and analyze the thinking that students' written work represents. Neither task is easy; students are not accustomed to communicating their thinking orally or in writing in math class, nor are teachers accustomed to hearing the mathematical thinking in the moment of teaching or responding appropriately to written work. Being unable to respond in the moment hinders opportunities to build on student ideas or deepen students' mathematical reasoning.

Workshop Models

This chapter outlines two different workshop formats: one for a full-day workshop and one for a two- to three-hour workshop.

Key understandings to be developed

Both workshop formats strive to develop the following ideas:

1. Effective math teachers have a deep understanding of the mathematical landscape—the big ideas, strategies, and models of the mathematics they teach.

2. Effective math teachers can predict student strategies and struggles to support student learning.

3. Effective math teachers pose *just-right* kinds of questions. Just-right questions engage or refocus students or help to clarify student thinking. Just-right questions are consciously chosen at varied levels of cognitive demand. Just-right questions can create the confusion or disequilibrium that opens and deepens student thinking.

4. Children's communications, both written and oral, are often difficult to interpret. Effective mathematics teachers have the tools to make explicit for the whole group the ideas implicit in one student's talk or writing.

5. Creating rich dialogue in a classroom requires teachers to have the right kind of talk tools in their pedagogical repertoire. Effective math teachers know when and how to use these tools to create an environment rooted in rich and vibrant discourse.

Context of the workshops

Before the workshop, assign the "Best Buy" problem to a random group of sixth-grade students. Make copies of four or five pieces of student work to show how various students solved the problem. At its simplest, the problem is as follows: *Which is the best buy, 12 items for $15 or 20 items for $23?*

This Best Buy problem can be used to assess the Number and Operations goal of the Curriculum Focal Points for grade 6 (adapted from NCTM [2006], p. 18). See problem 4, "Ratios," in this volume's chapter 3 for another version of this problem.

Grade 6 Curriculum Focal Points

Number and Operations: **Connecting ratio and rate to multiplication and division**

Students use simple reasoning about multiplication and division to solve ratio and rate problems (e.g., "If 5 items cost $3.75 and all items are the same price, then I can find the cost of 12 items by first dividing $3.75 by 5 to find out how much one item costs and then multiplying the cost of a single item by 12"). By viewing equivalent ratios and rates as deriving from, and extending, pairs of rows (or columns) in the multiplication table, and by analyzing simple drawings that indicate the relative sizes of quantities, students extend whole-number multiplication and division to ratios and rates. Thus, they expand the repertoire of problems that they can solve by using multiplication and division, and they build on their understanding of fractions to understand ratios. Students solve a wide variety of problems involving ratios and rates.

Teachers can also use this problem to assess students' prior knowledge and to make connections between a best-buy situation and concepts of proportionality in seventh grade and the slope of a linear equation in eighth grade (adapted from NCTM [2006], pp. 19–20).

Grade 7 Curriculum Focal Points

Number and Operations and Algebra and Geometry: **Developing an understanding of and applying proportionality, including similarity**

Students extend their work with ratios to develop an understanding of proportionality that they apply to solve single- and multistep problems in many contexts. They use ratio and proportionality to solve a wide variety of percent problems, including problems involving discounts, interest, taxes, tips, and percent increase or decrease. They also solve problems about similar objects (including figures) by using scale factors that relate corresponding lengths of the objects or by using the fact that relationships of lengths within an object are preserved in similar objects. Students graph proportional relationships and identify the unit rate as the slope of the related line. They distinguish proportional relationships ($y/x = k$, or $y = kx$) from other relationships, including inverse proportionality ($xy = k$, or $y = k/x$).

Grade 8 Curriculum Focal Points

Algebra: **Analyzing and representing linear functions and solving linear equations and systems of linear equations**

Students use linear functions, linear equations, and systems of linear equations to represent, analyze, and solve a variety of problems. They recognize a proportion ($y/x = k$, or $y = kx$) as a special case of a linear equation of the form $y = mx + b$, understanding that the constant of proportionality (k) is the slope and the resulting graph is a line through the origin. Students understand that the slope (m) of a line is a constant rate of change, so if the input, or x-coordinate, changes by a specific amount, a, the output, or y-coordinate, changes by the amount ma. Students translate among verbal, tabular, graphical, and algebraic representations of functions (recognizing that tabular and graphical representations are usually only partial representations), and they describe how such aspects of a function as slope and y-intercept appear in different representations. Students solve systems of two linear equations in two variables and relate the systems to pairs of lines that intersect, are parallel, or are the same line, in the plane. Students use linear equations, systems of linear equations, linear functions, and their understanding of the slope of a line to analyze situations and solve problems.

More important, this particular problem can reveal misconceptions and faulty reasoning. For example, the difference between the number of items in the two situations is equivalent to the difference in the cost—that is, 8 more items for 8 more dollars. Also, in each situation, the number of items is 3 fewer than the number of dollars. Students might successfully solve other Best Buy problems—but with misconceptions that would not be obvious from the solutions.

Workshop Model 1 (Full Day)

In this workshop, teachers spend the morning doing mathematics and the afternoon using student work to understand and further develop student mathematical knowledge. The goals of the workshop are for teachers to do the following:

1. Experience mathematics as *mathematizing* by participating in a carefully constructed, interactive mathematical experience
2. Develop and deepen the mathematical knowledge of students by becoming more skillful at analyzing and responding to student work

Facilitator Tip 1

The Best Buy problem on the surface may seem easy to participants. As participants work on the problem, be sure to challenge their thinking. For example, if they are finding a unit price, ask them whether they might have known which is the best buy *before* actually finishing the computation. For example, if one thinks about the distributive property—$15/12 = $12 + $3/12; $23/20 = $20 + $3/20— one is left comparing $3/12 and $3/20. Using a comparative kind of reasoning about fractions (if the numerators are the same, the greater the denominator and the smaller the quotient), one does not have to compute to know which is the best deal.

Exploring mathematics—morning (3 hours)

After welcoming participants and describing the goals and structure of the workshop, present the Best Buy problem:

The Best Buy Problem

The sixth-grade teachers need to buy T-shirts for field day, which is coming up soon. My neighborhood has two stores, Super-Sized Sales and Deep Discount Depot, having sales on T-shirts. Both stores sell the same kind of T-shirt but for different prices. Super-Sized Sales sells 12 T-shirts for $15; Deep Discount Depot sells 20 T-shirts for $23. Which store has the best buy?

Activity	Group size	Time
Participants solve the problem individually	Individual	5 minutes
Participants share their strategies in a small-group discussion	Small group (4–6)	15 minutes
Participants create a poster of the synthesis of their ideas—a coherent piece of mathematical writing	Return to small group	15 minutes
Gallery walk (see chapter 2)	Whole group	20 minutes
Activity	**Group size**	**Time**
Participants look at the comments and questions written by their peers and sort these comments into two piles: (1) helpful (e.g., questions and comments that would help revise the poster) and (2) not helpful.	Return to small group	15 minutes
Pick two or three pieces of work to use in a math share.	Facilitator	Done during postering
Math congress: facilitator models linking and developing mathematical ideas, creating disequilibrium, pushing thinking, and explicit use of particular talk tools. See chapter 2.	Whole group	20–30 minutes

Activity	Group size	Time
Participants write a reflection on their learning. Focus could be (1) questions I still have, (2) ideas I now understand, and (3) ideas I'd like to explore further.	Individual	10–15 minutes
Facilitator leads participants in a discussion of three aspects of the morning: (1) What facilitated learning? (2) How did communication (both written and oral) facilitate the development of mathematical thinking? (3) What specific tools the facilitator used to support discourse	Whole group	10 minutes
Chart participants' ideas. See Facilitator Tip 2.		

Facilitator Tip 2

Charts can be returned to at the end of the day as a tool to help participants summarize their learning and think about what their experiences as learners mean for how they will incorporate problem-solving strategies into their lessons, how they will engage their students in discussions and active listening, and how they will structure lessons to accommodate student self-reflection.

Analyzing and responding to student work—afternoon (3 hours)

Facilitator Tip 3

Teachers' ability to predict children's strategies is related to teachers' own content knowledge. When the range of adult strategies is narrow or algorithmic, you can assume that their ability to predict children's thinking will also be limited.

At this point in the workshop, do not try to "fix" this by asking them to think of other strategies or by giving them the strategies yourself. Returning to their predictions after they have looked at and analyzed student work is more powerful. They can then add to their own list of strategies, using children's strategies.

After reminding participants of the goals of the workshop and reviewing key points from the morning, ask participants to think about their students and what responses they would have to the Best Buy problem.

Activity	Group size	Time
Participants predict a range of strategies students could use to solve the problem. (See Facilitator Tip 3.)	Small group (4–6)	5–10 minutes
Facilitator collects and posts all strategies and then guides participants in a discussion of the developmental stages of the strategies. (1) What are the big ideas underlying each specific strategy? (2) How are those big ideas linked?	Whole group	30 minutes
Facilitator distributes copies of student work for the Best Buy problem. Participants analyze student work according to these criteria: (1) What big ideas are students using? (2) What struggles are students having? (3) What evidence supports your conclusions?	Individual	30 minutes
Facilitator analyzes student work with participants by using an Analyzing Student Work recording sheet, a template for which is at the end of this Professional Development Guide.	Whole group	20 minutes
Use student work to generate specific questions that might be asked to support student thinking.	Small group	30 minutes
Plan a math congress (see chapter 2): 1. Select specific pieces of student work. 2. Explain the rationale for each choice. 3. Explain how each choice could support the growth and development of all learners in the classroom. 4. Explain the mathematical goals of the congress. 5. Explain how the congress will develop the mathematical thinking of the range of learners in the classroom.	Small group	Done during postering
Create a Math Congress Recording Sheet with two columns (see the end of this Professional Development Guide for a template): one for the choice of student work and one for the rationale for that choice. Participants share their choices and rationales. Do not comment on participants' choices as they share. Once all participants have shared, ask them to think about what commonalities and differences their choices exhibit. See Facilitator Tip 4.		20–30 minutes

Facilitator Tip 4

The object of creating a chart of participant choices for a math congress is to help teachers think about children's strategies and how to use them to support and develop mathematical thinking.

Structuring a math share in a way that supports development of student thinking may be new to some teachers, who may think of the share in a math lesson as the time to "show" or get students to "see" a better strategy. But for students whose own constructions are markedly different, "showing" makes understanding harder. The further the shared strategy is from a child's own constructions, the more difficult the understanding.

Showing a correct strategy is not the same as mathematizing. To construct big ideas, children need to have many opportunities to mentally act on those ideas and be part of discussion where they share, explore, and resolve confusions and understandings. The teacher's ability to facilitate a mathematically rich conversation is essential in this phase. He or she must understand that confusion and disequilibrium are natural parts of learning.

The teacher's temptation to "fix it" (the "it" sometimes being the learner) or "show it" to the learner is powerful, and this workshop needs to address it directly. Such shortsighted impulses by teachers often heighten children's frustration, promote student silence, and ultimately deepen student confusion rather than understanding.

Workshop Model 2 (2–3 Hours)

The goal of this workshop is the same as the goal for the afternoon portion of workshop 1: to help teachers develop and deepen the mathematical knowledge of students by becoming more skillful at analyzing and responding to student work.

Part 1: So that participants can better analyze and discuss the mathematics involved in the Best Buy problem, give them the following allotments:

1. Five minutes to solve the problem on their own.

2. Five minutes to share their strategies in small groups.

3. Five minutes to share their strategies in a whole-group discussion. Be sure to highlight as many different strategies as possible, the mathematical reasons why they work, and how they may be related.

Part 2: Now that they have explored the mathematics of the Best Buy problem as learners, ask teachers to think about the problem from the student perspective:

1. Predict how many sixth graders in a class of twenty-six students would solve the problem: 25%? 50%? 100%?

2. Predict the possible strategies children might use. What big ideas underlie those strategies? If teachers' ability to predict the range of children's strategies is limited, do not worry about fixing this now. (See Facilitator Tip 3.)

3. Predict different ways that children might model the problem.

4. Using the list of children's strategies that participants have generated, ask them to predict children's potential struggles. (See the Analyzing Student Work Recording Sheet template at the end of this Professional Development Guide.)

Part 3: Distribute copies of your student work. Ask pairs of participants to think about how they would respond to the student work. Give partnered teams sticky notes so that they can record the comments or questions they would pose to students. Remind them that these comments or questions would be placed on student work and should be designed to do some or all of the following: (1) deepen student thinking, (2) highlight or work with misconceptions, and (3) refine children's informal solutions in ways that make their writing clearer.

Part 4: Pick one piece of student work and ask participants to share their comments or questions with the whole group. After recording these, ask participants to think about commonalities or differences in their questions, what might constitute a just-right question, and how certain kinds of questions might shift or refine students' mathematical thinking.

REFERENCES

Fosnot, Catherine Twomey, and Maarten Dolk. *Young Mathematicians at Work: Constructing Fractions, Decimals, and Percents.* Portsmouth, N.H.: Heinemann, 2007.

National Council of Teachers of Mathematics (NCTM). *Curriculum Focal Points for Prekindergarten through Grade 8 Mathematics: A Quest for Coherence.* Reston, Va.: NCTM, 2006.

Smith, Margaret Schwan, and Mary Kay Stein. "Selecting and Creating Mathematical Tasks: From Research to Practice." *Mathematics Teaching in the Middle School* 3 (February 1998): 344–50.

Stigler, James W., and James Hiebert. "Teaching Is a Cultural Activity." *American Educator* 22 (Winter 1998): 4–11.

Analyzing Student Work Recording Sheet

Student work #	Strategies	Big ideas	Models	Possible questions
1				
2				
3				
4				
5				
6				
7				
8				
9				
10				
11				
12				

Math Congress Recording Sheet

Share (student work in order of presentation)	Rationale for your share